Gin Cocktails Book

The 200 tastiest recipes

to make yourself

Randall Burch

Foreword

Welcome to the world of gin cocktails! In this book we have put together a selection of delicious gin cocktail recipes for you, including both classic mixed drinks and new, creative creations. We have made sure that there is something for every taste and also have a selection of non-alcoholic cocktails for those of you who want to or can do without alcohol.

Gin is a versatile and versatile juniper spirit that can be used in many different cocktails. From refreshing gin and tonics to complex, aromatic long drinks, there are countless ways you can use gin in cocktails.

We hope you enjoy trying out our recipes and that you discover new, delicious gin cocktails that you will enjoy mixing again and again.

Cheers!

Content

History of Gin

Gin originated in the 17th century in the Netherlands, where it was sold as a remedy for various ailments. The name "gin" is derived from the French word "genièvre", which means juniper. Juniper was one of the main ingredients of the original gin and gave it its characteristic aroma.

In the 18th century, gin became very popular, especially in England. It was also during this time that London Dry Gin was developed, which is still very common today. London Dry Gin is a high-proof gin made from juniper, citrus fruits and other botanical ingredients. It is dry and has a clear, fresh aroma.

Over the centuries, gin has been modified and developed again and again, so that today there are many different types of gin. Some gins are made with more juniper, others with less, some are sweeter, others drier. There are also gins that are enriched with different botanical ingredients, such as coriander, angelica root or rose petals.

Nowadays, gin is produced in many parts of the world and is a popular spirit for cocktails. It is often mixed with tonic water or other mixed drinks and is also suitable as a base for many long drinks. The gin boom of recent years has meant that there are now numerous small, independent gin distilleries producing experimental and innovative gins.

Overall, gin has a long and colourful history dating back to the 17th century. It is a versatile spirit that can be used in many different cocktails and is now popular all over the world.

Drinks

GIN TONIC/ GIN & TONIC

The gin and tonic is probably the best-known drink with gin. It is easy to mix, goes quickly and does not require many ingredients. This recipe is particularly suitable for beginners in mixing and drinking gin.

Ingredients for 1 jar:

Gin (dry gin is perfect for a gin and tonic)

Tonic Water

Ice cube

1 slice of cucumber, orange, lime or lemon

Preparation:

Take a long drink glass and fill it with ice cubes. You can choose whether you want to fill it to the brim or only put a few pieces in.

Now pour the gin and tonic water together into the glass on top of the ice cubes. This will cool the drink down more quickly.

3. last but not least, you can pimp the drink with a slice of cucumber, for example. Slices of orange, lime or lemon are also suitable for a light aroma.

Hint:

At the beginning, you will have noticed that there are no quantity specifications for this drink. You should determine the mixing ratio yourself as you see fit. Preferably, take a 1 to 1 mixture.

GIN TONIC COFFEE

Irish coffee after a meal or to wake up when celebrating was yesterday. Today, people are increasingly turning to gin and tonic coffee. Mixing the drink is almost as easy as with a gin and tonic.

Ingredients for 1 jar:

Gin (dry gin is also recommended here)

Tonic Water

Cold Brew Coffee

Ice cube

¼ lemon

1 coffee bean

Preparation:

Take a long drink glass and fill it with ice cubes. You can choose whether you want to fill it to the brim or only put a few pieces in.

Now pour the gin, Cold Brew Coffee and tonic water together into the glass on top of the ice cubes. This will cool the drink down more quickly.

Peel the lemon and decorate the peel on a toothpick. Alternatively, you can add a slice of lemon to your drink.

4. add the coffee bean.

Hint:

Again, there are no quantities, as it depends mainly on your own taste. Preferably 2 cl gin, 8 cl tonic water and 4 cl Cold Brew Coffee.

GIN SOUR

As the name suggests, the gin sour is drunk sour. For this, take the gin you like best and use freshly squeezed lemons for the lemon juice so as not to distort the aroma.

Ingredients for 1 jar:

5cl gin

3cl lemon juice

2cl sugar syrup

1 dash soda

You will also need a shaker.

Preparation:

1. put the gin, lemon juice and syrup in the shaker and shake the mixture.

Pour the mixture into a glass and add a little soda.

3. at the end, the drink can be decorated with a slice of lemon.

Hint:

Ice cubes are not desired in the original so as not to spoil the sour taste. A very similar recipe including ice cubes will follow.

GREEN SOUR

The Green Sour is a flavourful variation of the Gin Sour. This is one example of many ways you can create your own gin sour. Let your imagination and taste run wild.

Ingredients for 1 jar:

3 cl gin

3 cl woodruff syrup

2 cl lemon juice

Crushed ice

Optional shot of soda

You will also need a shaker.

Preparation:

The preparation here is very simple. You put everything together in the shaker and shake the drink until it becomes a little milky. Then pour the drink into a glass and enjoy it.

Hint:

You can use the Green Sour as a template for your own creations. Simply replace the woodruff syrup with a syrup of your choice.

HEMINGWAY SOUR

In addition to the gin sour and its variations, there is also the Hemingway Sour. Here, it is not syrup that is used, but grenadine.

Ingredients for 1 jar:

4 cl gin

3 cl lemon juice

2 cl grenadine

Ice cube

You will also need a shaker.

Preparation:

The preparation is more than simple. Everything is mixed together in a shaker and poured into a glass.

Hint:

There are also different variations of the Hemingway Sour. For example, you can fill it up with orange juice or decorate it with different fruits. Whatever tastes good is allowed.

GIN & JUICE

The Gin & Juice is also considered a classic and is very simple to make. You can vary the taste of this drink as much as you like. Basically, the following things apply here.

Ingredients for 1 jar:

4 cl gin

10-12 cl grape juice

2 cl soda (to taste)

1 cl fresh citrus juice (lime or lemon)

You will also need a stirring rod.

Preparation:

Fill the glass with ice cubes and pour the liquids on top. This will cool the drink down faster.

2. stir.

That's it.

Hint:

You can substitute any other juices for the grape juice, depending on your taste. Soda is not absolutely necessary to make a real Gin & Juice.

GIN BASIL SMASH

The Gin Basil Smash used to be called Gin Pesto.

Ingredients for 1 jar:

6 cl gin

A few basil leaves (depending on intensity)

2 cl lemon juice (preferably freshly squeezed)

2 cl sugar syrup

Ice cube

You will also need a shaker and a pestle.

Furthermore, a sieve is required.

Preparation:

First, put the basil leaves in the shaker with the sugar syrup and mix with the pestle.

Once this is done, add the gin and lemon juice.

Fill a glass with ice cubes and pour the mixture from the shaker through a sieve onto the ice cubes. This will cool the drink down faster.

GIN STRAWEBERRY SMASH

The Gin Strawberry Smash logically has a completely different taste than the Gin Basil Smash. The cocktail tastes a little sweeter and has nothing in common with the taste of the old Gin Pesto.

Ingredients for 1 jar:

8 cl gin

1 cl lime juice (preferably freshly squeezed)

1 cl sugar syrup

4 strawberries

Soda

Ice cube

A shaker is also needed. Furthermore, a sieve is required.

Preparation:

1. mix the gin, lime juice and syrup with ice cubes in a shaker.

Fill a glass with ice cubes and three strawberries.

Pour the mixture from the shaker into the glass through the sieve.

4. the drink is topped up with soda.

The last strawberry is used for decoration.

GIN BUCK

The Gin Buck is a strong and at the same time fruity drink.

Ingredients for 1 jar:

50 ml gin

10 ml lemon juice (freshly squeezed if possible)

100 ml ginger ale

Ice cube

Preparation:

1. to start, fill the glass with ice cubes.

In the second step, add the gin and lemon juice to the ice cubes. This will cool the drink down faster.

Add the ginger ale.

4. stir, ready!

Hint:

You can also add a slice of lemon to the drink. This is best done after the second step to taste the light aroma of the lemon.

GIN DAISY

The Gin Daisy is very similar to the Hemingway Sour. However, the cane sugar adds a certain sweetness. In addition, the drink is lovingly decorated with sweet fruits.

Ingredients for 1 jar:

4 cl gin

2 cl lemon juice (freshly squeezed if possible)

1 cl grenadine

1 tsp cane sugar

Cocktail cherries

Soda

You will also need a shaker.

Preparation:

The preparation is exceedingly simple, which is why the steps are not worth listing. Because: You put everything except the cherries and the soda into the shaker and mix everything together before you tip it into a glass. You can now add soda to taste. Decorate the drink with cocktail cherries and the Gin Daisy is ready.

GIN FIZZ

Let's move on to the Gin Fizz, which is very similar to the Gin Sour, as already mentioned. The differences are vanishingly small and can ultimately only be noticed when drinking. The Gin Fizz contains more soda than the Gin Sour, which is why it tingles more due to the carbonic acid. In addition, ice cubes are added in this recipe, which is why the Gin Sour tastes more like the chosen gin than the Gin Fizz.

Ingredients for 1 jar:

5 cl gin

3 cl lemon juice (preferably freshly squeezed)

2 cl sugar syrup

10 cl soda

Ice cube

You will also need a shaker.

Preparation:

1. put the gin, lemon juice, syrup and a few ice cubes in the shaker and shake the mixture.

Pour the mixture into a glass filled with ice cubes and add the soda.

3. decorate as desired.

ALABAMA FIZZ

The Alabama Fizz is a refreshing medium-sweet drink.

Ingredients for 1 jar:

2 cl gin

1 cl Crème de Menthe (or also called peppermint liqueur)

1 cl lemon juice

1 cl sugar syrup

Soda

Ice cube

You will also need a shaker.

Preparation:

Put all the ingredients except the soda in the shaker and shake.

Pour the mixture into a glass and top up with fresh cold soda to taste.

3. decorate as desired. Lemon slices are a good choice here.

GOLDEN FIZZ

Another fizz is the Golden Fizz with its refined ingredients.

Ingredients for 1 jar:

4 cl gin

2 cl lemon juice (preferably freshly squeezed)

2 tsp sugar (optionally 2 cl sugar syrup)

1 egg yolk

Soda

Ice cube

A shaker is also needed.

Preparation:

1. put everything except the soda in the shaker and shake.

Transfer the mixture into a glass.

Fill up the drink with soda.

4. sit back and enjoy.

SLOE GIN FIZZ

The Sloe Gin Fizz is a harder drink than the normal Gin Fizz due to the mix of two gin varieties.

Ingredients:

2 cl Sloe Gin

3 cl gin (dry gin is best)

3 cl lemon juice (preferably freshly squeezed)

1 cl sugar syrup

Ice cube

Soda

You will also need a shaker.

Preparation:

Shake everything except the soda in a shaker.

Fill a glass with more ice cubes and add the mix.

Add soda according to taste.

4. lemons or limes are suitable for decoration.

VIOLET FIZZ

The Violet Fizz is a special drink that you don't see very often. The special thing about it is the violet aroma.

Ingredients for 1 jar:

2 cl gin

1 cl Crème de Violette

1-2 cl lemon juice (according to taste)

1 cl sugar syrup

Soda

Ice cube

Furthermore, you need a shaker.

Preparation:

Add all ingredients except soda to the shaker and shake.

Pour the mixture into a glass and top up with fresh cold soda to taste.

3. decoration is not necessary. A purple blossom nevertheless fits perfectly.

WATERMELON GIN FIZZ

The Watermelon Gin Fizz tastes like summer.

Ingredients for 1 jar:

40 ml gin

1 lime

190 grams watermelon (seeded)

10 g cane sugar

60 ml mineral water

You will also need a blender. You will also need a sieve.

Preparation:

Squeeze the lime and then cut it into slices.

Chill the melon before preparing it. Get out the flesh and remove the seeds. Then puree the melon.

Pour the puree through the sieve into a glass and add the sugar, lime juice and gin.

4. at the end, the drink is filled with mineral water and is ready to drink.

Hint:

If the melon is not cold enough for you, you can add ice cubes.

Decorate the cocktail - if at all - with mint leaves.

GIN MULE OR GIN GIN MULE

This drink is the variant of the probably better known Moscow Mule, whereby the Gin (gin) Mule is made with the juniper-containing liquor.

Ingredients for 1 jar:

5 cl gin

6-8 mint leaves

2.5 cl lime juice (preferably freshly squeezed)

3 cl sugar syrup

3 cl Ginger Beer

Ice cube

You also need a shaker. A sieve is also necessary.

Preparation:

Pour the mint, lime juice and sugar syrup into the shaker, crush so that the mint leaves release their juice, and stir.

Next, add the gin and a few ice cubes to the shaker and shake the mixture.

Fill a glass with fresh ice cubes.

Pour through the sieve into the glass.

In the last step, fill the glass with the ginger beer. You can decide for yourself whether the 3 cl is enough for you.

MUNICH MULE

The Munich Mule was initially a local variation of the Gin Gin Mule. In the meantime, however, the Munich Mule is known everywhere, at least in Germany.

Ingredients for 1 jar:

6 cl gin

1/2 fresh lime

14 cl Ginger Beer

Ice cube

Cucumber

Preparation:

You might think that it is difficult to prepare. However, this is not the case. All you have to do is squeeze the lime and put everything together in a cup. The cucumber is used for decoration.

GIN ORANGE

The Gin Orange is a fruity and easy to prepare long drink.

Ingredients for 1 jar:

4 cl gin

2 cl orange juice (preferably freshly squeezed)

Ice cube

1/2 orange

You will also need a shaker. You will also need a sieve.

Preparation:

1. put everything except the orange in the shaker and shake the mixture.

Pour the mixture through a sieve into a glass.

The orange is then used to decorate the glass.

Hint:

A small but delicious variation of Gin Orange can be achieved by adding a shot of sparkling wine.

GIN RICKEY

The Gin Rickey is a simple drink that people like to serve on a formal evening.

Ingredients for 1 jar:

4 cl gin

2 cl lime juice (preferably freshly squeezed)

1 cl sugar syrup (if desired)

Soda

Ice cube

2 lime slices

Preparation:

1. put two ice cubes in the glass.

Mix the gin and lime juice together in the glass on the ice cubes. This will cool the drink down more quickly.

If the sugar syrup is desired, pour it into the glass and stir the mixture.

4. then add the lime slices.

GIN SUNRISE

The Gin Sunrise is the counterpart to the Tequila Sunrise, but tastes a little more tart.

Ingredients for 1 jar:

6 cl gin

10 cl orange juice (preferably freshly squeezed)

2 cl grenadine

A few drops of lemon juice (preferably from a fresh lemon)

Ice cube

You will also need a shaker.

Preparation:

Fill the shaker with ice cubes, orange juice, the gin and a few drops of lemon juice and shake.

Pour into a glass.

Carefully add the grenadine at the end.

GIN SWITCHEL

The Switchel is originally a non-alcoholic drink. However, it also tastes good with gin, which is why the Gin Switchel is now a well-known drink, although it has many ingredients and is not quite as easy to mix.

Ingredients for 1 jar:

30 grams ginger, peeled **and grated**

1 tbsp maple syrup

10 ml apple cider vinegar

Lemon juice (freshly squeezed from half a lemon)

20 ml gin

50 ml mineral water

Mint and rosemary

Ice cube

You will also need a sieve.

Preparation:

Bring water to the boil and add the ginger. Bring to the boil and leave to infuse for a while.

Mix the maple syrup, apple cider vinegar and lemon juice. Add the ginger water through a sieve and chill. The switchel is now ready.

After the mixture has cooled down, ice cubes are poured into a glass. Now pour in the gin and 60 ml of the switchel and top up with mineral water.

4. mint or rosemary are suitable for decoration.

ABSINTHE PASSION FRUIT

With the name, you might think that there is no gin in this drink. Far from it. It is the gin that makes the Absinthe Maracuja what it is. Moreover, the preparation is wonderfully simple.

Ingredients for 1 jar:

4 cl absinthe

2 cl dry gin

10 cl passion fruit nectar

Ice cube

You will also need a sieve.

Preparation:

Pour the alcohol and ice into a glass and stir well.

Fill another glass with ice cubes.

Pour the mixture through a sieve into the glass filled with ice cubes. This cools the drink more quickly.

4. add the nectar afterwards.

Hint:

Not only oranges or a cocktail cherry are suitable for decoration. A kiwi is just as colourful as it is sophisticated.

ABSINTHE KAMIKAZE

This cocktail is mixed with very many different alcoholic drinks, which is why the absinthe Kamikaze lives up to its name.

Ingredients for 1 jar:

1 cl absinthe

1 cl bourbon whiskey

1 cl Cointreau

1 cl gin

1 cl brown rum

1 cl tequila

1 cl vodka

1 cl grenadine

Ice cube

A sieve is also needed.

Preparation:

1. chill an empty glass before you start.

2. put ice cubes with all sorts except absinthe into a container and stir vigorously.

3. pour the mixture through the sieve into the pre-cooled glass.

Add the absinthe. It is best to add it slowly over the inside of the glass.

Light and leave to burn briefly.

ATTENTION: Be sure to extinguish the flame before drinking. Danger of burns!

ALABAMA SLAMMER

The Alabama Slammer is a spicy drink that should be drunk immediately after preparation.

Ingredients for 1 jar:

2 cl gin

3 cl Southern Comfort

4 cl orange juice (preferably freshly squeezed)

2 cl amaretto

Ice cube

Preparation:

The preparation is simple. Fill a glass with ice cubes and add all the other ingredients. This will cool the drink down faster. Stir briefly. Et Voila!

Hint:

Depending on your taste, you can add a shot of vodka to the drink.

ANGELS FACE / ANGELS FACE / ANGEL`S FACE

The Angels Face drink is a very simple, good-tasting drink.

Ingredients for 1 jar:

2 cl gin

2 cl Apricot Brandy

2 cl Calvados

Ice cube

1 cocktail cherry

You will also need a shaker.

Furthermore, you need a sieve.

Preparation:

1. add everything together in the shaker and mix the drink properly.

Pour the mixture through a sieve into a glass.

3. cocktail cherries are suitable for decoration.

APEROL ITALIAN SLING

The Aperol Italian Sling is a variation of the better known Singapore Sling, which I will also discuss below.

Ingredients for 1 jar:

1 cl sugar syrup

3 cl Aperol

3 cl gin

2 cl lemon juice (preferably freshly squeezed)

1 cl orange juice (preferably freshly squeezed)

5 cl soda

Ice cube

You will also need a shaker.

Preparation:

Shake all the ingredients except the ice cubes and soda well in a shaker.

Fill a glass with ice cubes. This will cool the drink down faster.

Pour the mixture over the ice cubes and then add the soda.

SAIGON SLING

The Saigon Sling is also a variation of the Singapore Sling.

Ingredients for 1 jar:

2 cl gin

1 cl Cointreau

1 cl passion fruit syrup

3 cl pineapple juice (preferably freshly squeezed)

4 cl bitter lemon

Ice cube

Lime

You will also need a shaker.

Preparation:

Mix the gin, Cointreau, passion fruit syrup and pineapple juice with ice cubes in a shaker.

Shake the mixture until some foam is formed.

Now pour the mix into a glass filled with ice cubes. This will cool the drink down faster.

4. Then add bitter lemon.

5. stir.

Decorate with a slice of lime.

SINGAPORE SLING

The Singapore Sling is a legendary drink that was once invented in Singapore. There are now several variations of the Singapore Sling, which is why other recipes may have a different focus than mine. Below you will find my favourite recipe of the exotic drink.

Ingredients for 1 jar:

3 cl gin

2 cl Cherry Brandy

1 cl Cointreau

1 cl DOM Bénédictine

1 cl grenadine

10 cl pineapple juice (preferably freshly squeezed)

1 - 2 cl lime juice (preferably freshly squeezed and according to taste)

1 dash Angostura bitters

Ice cube

2 pieces of pineapple and a cocktail cherry

You will also need a shaker.

Preparation:

Put all the liquids in a shaker and shake until it foams.

Pour the mixture slowly into a glass filled with ice cubes so that the foam collects on the surface and a head of foam remains. This cools the drink more quickly.

Decorate traditionally with pineapple chunks and a cocktail cherry.

SOHO SLING

The Soho Sling is the last sling I will present here. It is considered a winter drink, although it is drunk with ice cubes. Moreover, the drink comes from New York and not, as some think, from London.

Ingredients for 1 jar:

5 cl gin

1 cl lime juice (freshly squeezed)

5 cl Ginger Beer

4 cl naturally cloudy apple juice

Ice cube

2 thyme sprigs

3 thin apple slices

Preparation:

1. fill a glass with ice cubes.

Add the gin, lime juice and apple juice. This will cool the drink down faster.

Finally, add the ginger beer and stir the drink.

Rub the thyme sprigs between your hands and add them to the jar.

Finally, place the apple slices on the rim of the glass.

AUQA VELVA

Aqua Velva is a cocktail for the taste buds and the eyes.

Ingredients for 1 jar:

4 cl vodka

4 cl gin

4 cl Blue Curacao

20 cl lemonade

Ice cube

You will also need a shaker.

Preparation:

Pour the alcohol with ice cubes into the shaker and shake.

Pour the mixture into a glass and add the lemonade at the end.

AVIATION

The Aviation is a Sour Cocktail.

Ingredients for 1 jar:

6 cl gin

1 cl maraschino

1 cl Crème de Violette

3 cl lemon juice (preferably freshly squeezed)

Ice cube

Cocktail cherries

You will also need a shaker. A sieve is also necessary.

Preparation:

Put everything except the cocktail cherries in the shaker and shake well.

Then stir until the drink looks pale blue.

Pour through a sieve into an empty glass.

Decorate with cocktail cherries.

BLUE LADY

The Blue Lady drink is very similar to Aqua Velva, but is prepared without vodka and real juice instead of soda.

Ingredients for 1 jar:

4 cl gin

2 cl Blue Curacao

2 cl lemon juice (preferably freshly squeezed)

Ice cube

A shaker is also required.

Preparation:

The preparation is very simple. Simply put everything together in the shaker, shake and pour into a glass.

Hint:

For decoration, you can garnish the glass with lemon slices. Another possibility, moreover a little more classic, would be to choose a cocktail cherry in the glass.

BACARDI SPECIAL

This cocktail is very easy to prepare, which is why it is also suitable for beginners to mix.

Ingredients for 1 jar:

1 cl grenadine

1 cl lime juice (preferably freshly squeezed)

1 cl gin

4 cl white rum

Ice cubes.

You will also need a shaker.

Preparation:

1. chill a glass before preparation.

Add all ingredients to the shaker and shake well.

3. then pour into the cold glass.

BEE`S KNEES

Bee`s Knees is also called Midnight in Paris and has its origins in the French metropolis. At the same time, there is a theory that the origin of this drink lies far in the past and that gin, which was not as pure and delicious back then as it is by today`s standards, had to be stretched and sweetened in order to be able to drink it. In the meantime, it is believed that both theories are true.

Ingredients for 1 jar:

6 cl gin

3 tsp honey

2 cl lemon juice (preferably freshly squeezed)

Ice cube

You will also need a shaker.

Preparation:

1. chill a glass in advance.

First put the gin with the honey into the shaker and work this mixture until the honey dissolves. Preferably by means of stirring and not shaking.

Once step 2 is complete, add the lemon juice and ice cubes and shake.

Pour the mixture into the chilled glass.

Hint:

For decoration, you can attach lemon peels to the rim of the glass.

BIG BEN

The Big Ben is a fruity fresh summer cocktail.

Ingredients for 1 jar:

5 cl gin

4 cl orange juice (preferably freshly squeezed)

2 cl lemon juice (freshly squeezed juice works very well)

1 cl grenadine

10 cl bitter lemon

Ice cube

You will also need a shaker and a sieve.

Preparation:

Put the gin in the shaker with the juices, syrup and a few ice cubes and shake well.

Fill a glass with ice cubes and pour the mix through the strainer.

Top up the drink with bitter lemon.

Hint:

Orange slices can be used as decoration.

BLACKBERRY PEACH BRAMBLE

The Blackberry Peach Bramble is a fruity cocktail that is easy to mix despite the many ingredients.

Ingredients for 1 jar:

90 ml lemonade

45 ml gin

30 ml peach pulp

15 ml crème de cassis

6 pcs. Blackberries (blackberry syrup is also fine)

Mint leaves and a piece of lemon

Ice cube

You will also need a shaker. A blender is also an advantage here.

Preparation:

Mix the peach pulp with the blackberries, preferably in a blender. Otherwise you can also mash everything.

2. then add the puree to the shaker with the lemonade, gin and ice cubes and shake everything well.

Pour the mix into a glass filled with ice cubes and then add the cassis.

4. the mint leaves and the piece of lemon, or alternatively a slice of lemon, serve as garnish.

BLUE BIRD

The Blue Bird looks beautiful and has a very special taste. The preparation is extremely simple.

Ingredients for 1 jar:

1 sugar cube

1 cl Blue Curacao

1 cl dry gin

1 cl Triple Sec

8 cl champagne

Preparation:

There are only two preparation levels for the Blue Bird.

First, pour the Blue Curacao over the sugar cube. Then add the rest.

BLUE DIAMOND

There are countless recipes for the Blue Diamond. Some are alcohol-free, others can be found without adding gin. However, I have chosen the gin variant, as it belongs in this book for completeness on the one hand and tastes wonderfully sparkling on the other.

Ingredients for 1 jar:

2 cl gin

2 cl Blue Curacao

2 cl lemon juice (preferably freshly squeezed)

6 cl sparkling wine

You will also need a shaker.

Preparation:

1. put all the ingredients except the sparkling wine in the shaker and shake it.

Pour the mixture into a glass and finally add the sparkling wine.

BLUE MONDAY

The Blue Monday is also part of our collection of blue cocktails and is extremely easy to make.

Ingredients for 1 jar:

2 cl gin

4 cl Cointreau

1 cl Blue Curacao

Soda

Ice cube

Preparation:

Fill a glass with ice and add the gin and Cointreau. This will cool the drink down more quickly.

Fill up the mixture with soda.

Then add the Blue Curacao and stir.

BLUE MONDAY TONIC

The Blue Monday Tonic is a variation of the Blue Monday, but tastes more bitter as the soda is replaced with tonic water.

Ingredients for 1 jar:

2 cl gin

4 cl Cointreau

1 cl Blue Curacao

Tonic Water

Preparation:

1. chill a glass before you start mixing.

Pour the gin and the Cointreau into the cold glass.

Fill the mixture with tonic water.

Then add the Blue Curacao and stir.

BOMBAY CRUSHED

This cocktail was developed by the Bombay Sapphire Gin brand to create its own drink. Today, it can be mixed with various types of gin.

Ingredients for 1 jar:

6 cl Gin (Besides Bombay Sapphire Gin, London Gin is also suitable)

6 kumquats

Juice 1 lime

2 bar spoons cane sugar

Crushed ice

You will also need a shaker.

Preparation:

1. chill a glass before you start mixing.

Place the kumquats in halves in the shaker with the cane sugar and mash.

Then add the rest and shake vigorously and for a long time.

Pour the mixture into the cold glass.

BOND`S MARTINI

Shaken, not stirred - that's what James Bond says. In fact, this drink is stirred when it is prepared outside the films.

Ingredients for 1 jar:

5 cl Dry Gin

3 cl vodka

1 cl Quinquina

Ice cube

Preparation:

1. put a glass in the freezer before you start mixing.

2. put all the ingredients together and stir.

Once the glass is frosted, pour the mix into it.

Hint:

Decorate the cocktail with a lemon zest.

BRAMBLE

The Bramble is fruity, but not sweet and easy to prepare.

Ingredients for 1 jar:

5 cl gin

2 cl lemon juice (preferably freshly squeezed)

1 cl sugar syrup

Ice cube

8 blackberries

Preparation:

1. first put up to 6 blackberries in a glass and crush them.

Then add the ice cubes. Pour the remaining ingredients on top of the ice cubes. This cools the drink down more quickly.

Stir briefly.

4. use the last 2 blackberries for decoration.

BRONX

The Bronx Cocktail is a medium-strength drink that originated in New York.

Ingredients for 1 jar:

4 cl gin

2 cl Vermouth rosso

2 cl Vermouth dry

4 cl orange juice (preferably freshly squeezed)

Ice cube

You will also need a shaker. You will also need a sieve.

Preparation:

The preparation is extremely simple. Put everything together in a shaker, shake and pour into a glass via the strainer.

Hint:

To make a nice rare sight, the drink is often decorated with a dried blood orange slice and a sprig of rosemary.

CAMPARI FLIP

The Campari Flip is a tart drink, which may seem a little strange at first, as you have to work with an egg yolk here.

Ingredients for 1 jar:

4 cl Campari

1 cl gin

4 cl orange juice (preferably freshly squeezed)

1 egg yolk

Ice cube

You will also need a shaker. A (bar) strainer is also necessary.

Preparation:

The preparation is very simple. Put everything together in the shaker, shake it and pour the mix over the strainer into a glass.

CARUSO

The Caruso is convincing from its appearance alone and tastes very refreshing.

Ingredients for 1 jar:

30 ml gin

10 ml green mint liqueur (crème de menthe)

20 ml dry vermouth (Vermouth Dry)

Ice cube

You will also need a shaker.

Preparation:

1. put all the ingredients in the shaker and shake it.

2. pour the mix into a glass.

Hint:

Peppermint leaves are suitable for decoration.

CHICAGO FREESTYLE

The Chicago Freestyle contains many different ingredients, but is very easy to prepare. But beware, it is a strong cocktail.

Ingredients for 1 jar:

2 cl vodka

2 cl gin

2 cl white rum

2 cl Southern Comfort (whiskey liqueur)

2 cl Blue Curacao

2 cl lime syrup

2 cl lemon juice (preferably freshly squeezed)

2 cl pineapple juice (preferably freshly squeezed)

4 cl orange juice (preferably freshly squeezed)

Ice cube

You will also need a shaker.

Preparation:

It is very easy to mix the Chicago Freestyle. Put everything together in the shaker, shake it and serve the cocktail in a fresh glass.

CLARIDGE

The Claridge is a fruity dry drink.

Ingredients for 1 jar:

20 ml gin

10 ml Apricot Brandy

20 ml dry vermouth (Vermouth Dry)

10 ml Triple Sec

Ice cube

You will also need a shaker.

Preparation:

1. put all the ingredients in the shaker and shake it.

2. then pour the mix into a glass and serve the drink.

CLOVER CLUB

The Clover Club cocktail stirs up discussions in the cocktail world, as there is no consensus on whether raspberry syrup belongs as an ingredient or not. Personally, I find it tastier with syrup, but decide for yourself.

Ingredients for 1 jar:

6 cl gin

3 cl lemon juice (preferably freshly squeezed)

1 cl raspberry syrup

3 raspberries

1 egg white

Ice cube

You also need a shaker. A sieve is also necessary.

Preparation:

1. chill a glass before preparation.

First put the raspberries in the shaker and grind.

Then add the rest and shake.

Filter out the ice cubes through the sieve and shake again until the drink foams.

Finally, pour the mix into the cool glass.

Hint:

If you want to decorate, you can add raspberries.

COCO LOCO

The Coco Loco has many variations to be prepared. In this book, I will of course introduce you to the one with gin.

Ingredients for 1 jar:

3 cl gin

12 cl pineapple juice (preferably freshly squeezed)

3 cl Batida de Coco

6 cl Cream of Coconut

3 cl tequila

5 cl rum (preferably white rum)

3 cl lemon juice (preferably freshly squeezed)

Ice cube

You also need a shaker. A sieve is also necessary.

Preparation:

1. chill a glass before preparing.

Put all the ingredients in the shaker and shake vigorously.

3. pour the mixture through the sieve into the cold glass.

Hint:

For a real eye-catcher, you can wrap a coconut so that it becomes a drinking vessel. In addition, you can decorate the drink well with pineapple slices.

CRANBERRY COOLER

Some people will know the Cranberry Cooler as a non-alcoholic drink. However, there is also a version with gin, which I present to you here.

Ingredients for 1 jar:

6 cl gin

2 cl cranberry syrup

12 cl orange juice (preferably freshly squeezed)

Ice cube

Preparation:

Making the colourful cocktail is extremely simple. Put everything together in a glass, stir the mixture and the drink is ready.

CRANBERRY GIN

At first glance, the Cranberry Gin seems very similar to the Cranberry Cooler. They are similar, but the cranberry gin is mixed with lemon juice instead of orange juice, and we use cranberry juice and not syrup. Furthermore, the quantities differ considerably.

Ingredients for 1 jar:

2 cl gin

12 cl cranberry juice

2 cl lemon juice (preferably freshly squeezed)

Crushed ice

Preparation:

Making the drink is extremely simple. Put everything together in a glass, stir the mixture and enjoy.

CREMA GIN

The Crema Gin is our first drink with egg liqueur. The mixture with lemon juice gives it a nice tart taste.

Ingredients for 1 jar:

4 cl gin

2 cl eggnog

1 cl lemon juice (preferably freshly squeezed)

10 cl tonic water

Ice cube

1 lemon slice

Preparation:

First, mix the egg liqueur with the lemon juice.

2. then add the gin and a few ice cubes to mix everything together.

Fill a glass with more ice cubes and pour the mix over it.

4. at the end, top up the drink with the tonic water.

Add the lemon slice to the glass for decoration.

CUCUMBER FROG

Nowadays, many things are decorated with cucumbers. Most of the time you'll find a slice of cucumber in a glass of water, but have you ever heard of cucumber in gin? It's certainly not all that surprising, but the Cucumber Frog will certainly push you to the edge of your imagination. Because it also contains wasabi.

Ingredients for 1 jar:

6 cl gin

2 cl basil syrup

1 tsp wasabi paste

10 cucumber slices

Ice cube

Preparation:

The preparation is extremely simple. Just put all the ingredients together and stir the mixture.

Hint:

If the cocktail is too strong for you, you can top it up with soda, or optionally add more cucumber.

DERBY

Derby is a fruity drink that does not taste too sweet or artificial due to the fresh juices.

Ingredients for 1 jar:

4 cl gin

8 cl passion fruit juice (preferably freshly squeezed)

1 cl grenadine

1 cl lemon juice (preferably freshly squeezed)

Ice cube

You will also need a shaker. A sieve is also necessary.

Preparation:

The preparation of this drink is extremely simple.

Put all the ingredients in the shaker and shake vigorously.

Pour the mixture through the sieve into a glass filled with fresh ice cubes.

Hint:

You can decorate the drink with a slice of lemon.

DIRTY MARTINI

In a gin recipe book, the Dirty Martini is a must.

Ingredients for 1 jar:

6 cl gin (preferably London Dry Gin)

2 cl dry vermouth (Vermouth Dry)

1 cl olive brine

1 Olive

Ice cube

Preparation:

1. place a jar in the freezer before starting.

When the glass is icy, put all the ingredients except the olive into a glass and stir.

3. add the olive as decoration.

Hint:

The Dirty Martini is also simply called Martini.

DRY MARTINI

The Dry Martini is very similar to the Dirty Martini, but still needs a lemon as a finish.

Ingredients for 1 jar:

6cl gin

1 cl dry vermouth (Vermouth Dry)

Ice cube

Lemon

You will also need a (bar) strainer.

Preparation:

1. chill the glass before preparation - not in the freezer as with the Dirty Martini.

Pour the gin and vermouth into a glass filled with ice and stir well.

3. then pour the mixture through the sieve into the chilled glass.

4. spray with a few squirts of lemon.

Hint:

For decoration, either a slice of lemon or the more familiar variant: an olive is suitable.

GIBSON MARTINI

The Gibson Martini is also very similar to the drinks mentioned above. Here too, however, there is a small variation that makes the martini unique.

Ingredients for 1 jar:

6 cl Dry Gin

2 cl dry vermouth (Vermouth Dry)

Ice cube

1 to 3 silver onions

You will also need a sieve

Preparation:

1. place a jar in the freezer before starting.

2. mix liquids over ice in a glass and stir vigorously.

3. pour the mixture through the sieve into the iced glass.

4. at the end, decorate the drink with the silver onions.

HEDGEHOG MARTINI

The Hedgehog Martini is one of the few that is shaken instead of stirred. Freely according to James Bond`s motto.

Ingredients for 1 jar:

6 cl gin (use a spicy variety here)

2 cl vodka

2 cl absinthe

Ice cube

You will also need a shaker.

Preparation:

1. chill a glass before preparation.

Add all ingredients to the shaker and shake vigorously.

Pour the mixture into the chilled glass.

PERFECT MARTINI

The Perfect Martini is, as the name suggests, perfect. You can decide for yourself whether this is really the case.

Ingredients for 1 jar:

4 cl gin

1 cl dry vermouth (Vermouth Dry)

1 cl red vermouth (Vermouth Rosso)

¼ lemon

Ice cube

You will also need a sieve.

Preparation:

1. mix the different drinks in a glass filled with ice cubes and stir.

Pour the mixture through a sieve into an empty glass.

Add a squeeze of the lemon over the drink.

Decorate with a slice of lemon.

SMOKEY MARTINI / SMOKY MARTINI

The Smokey Martini contains whiskey, which is why the addition Smokey was chosen.

Ingredients for 1 jar:

5 cl gin

1 cl Scotch whiskey

1 cl dry vermouth (Vermouth Dry)

Ice cube

Preparation:

1. chill a glass before preparation.

2. once the jar is cold, pour in all the ingredients and stir well.

Hint:

The vermouth is not in every recipe, but I personally find that it adds a smoky note to the drink. Try for yourself what suits you better.

SWEET MARTINI

The Sweet Martini is, as the name suggests, a sweet variation of the normal martini.

Ingredients for 1 jar:

4 cl gin

2 cl red vermouth (Vermouth Rosso)

Ice cube

Cocktail cherry

You will also need a (bar) sieve.

Preparation:

1. put the gin and vermouth in a glass with ice cubes and stir the mixture.

Pour over the sieve into a glass.

3. cocktail cherries are excellent for decoration because of their sweetness.

EARL GREY MARTEANI / EARL GREY MARTINI

As the name suggests, this cocktail is mixed with Earl Grey tea, making it a very unconventional blend.

Ingredients for 1 jar:

5 cl gin

1 tea bag Earl Grey

3 cl lemon juice (preferably freshly squeezed)

2 cl sugar syrup

1 egg white

Ice cube

You will also need a shaker. You will also need a (bar) strainer.

Preparation:

Add the tea bag to the gin and leave to infuse for about an hour.

2. meanwhile, chill a glass.

3. then the mixture can go into the shaker. Add the lemon juice, sugar syrup and egg white with ice cubes and shake everything vigorously.

Pour the drink through the strainer into the chilled glass.

DOLLY

The Dolly Cocktail is a simple but delicious cocktail.

Ingredients for 1 jar:

2 cl gin

3 cl white vermouth (Vermouth Bianco)

3 cl passion fruit juice (preferably freshly squeezed)

Ice cube

You will also need a shaker. A (bar) strainer is also necessary.

Preparation:

1. put all the ingredients in the shaker and shake vigorously.

Pour the mixture into the jar through a sieve.

Hint:

You can use a piece of passion fruit as decoration, or serve a cocktail cherry.

DRUNKEN LADY

The Drunken Lady could easily make you think of Bloody Mary. You will see why.

Ingredients for 1 jar:

3 cl gin

2 cl vodka

2 cl Blue Curacao

3 cl sparkling wine

1 cl tomato juice

Preparation:

The preparation is very simple. Put everything together in a glass and stir. You have an interesting mixture.

ELECTRIC ICE TEA

The Electric Ice Tea is a blue cocktail with many ingredients, but simple to prepare.

Ingredients for 1 jar:

3 cl gin

3 cl rum

3 cl vodka

1 cl tequila

1 cl Triple Sec

9 cl lemonade

Ice cube

You will also need a shaker.

Preparation:

Put all the alcohols in the shaker, add ice cubes and shake the mix.
Then pour it into a glass and fill it up with lemonade. If you want to decorate, a slice of lemon is suitable.

LONG ISLAND ICED TEA / LONG ISLAND ICE TEA

The Long Island Iced Tea is one of my favourite cocktails and a real classic that is known all over the world. Why not give it a try too?

Ingredients for 1 jar:

2 cl gin

2 cl vodka

2 cl white rum

2 cl tequila

2 cl Triple Sec

2 cl sugar cane syrup

2 cl lemon juice (preferably freshly squeezed) - lime juice is also an option

Cola

Ice cube

Lemon or lime

Preparation:

Despite the many ingredients, the preparation is simple. Put everything the gin, vodka, rum, tequila, triple sec, syrup and fruit juice in a glass with ice cubes. Top it off with cola and stir.

For decoration, you can choose lemon or lime slices, both also work.

Note: There is no gin in some Long Island Iced Tea recipes. I consider it complete only with this.

ELECTRIC POISON

Electric Poison is an extraordinary drink that is also a real eye-catcher. Unique in taste.

Ingredients for 1 jar:

4 cl gin

2 cl woodruff syrup

2 cl violet syrup

4 cl lime juice (preferably freshly squeezed)

Ice cube

A shaker is also necessary

Preparation:

1. put all ingredients without ice cubes into the shaker.

2. after shaking, pour into a glass filled with egg cubes.

Hint:

You can also top up the drink with ginger ale. Taste what you like.

FIVE O`CLOCK

The Five O`Clock is a spicy cocktail with a very simple preparation.

Ingredients for 1 jar:

2 cl gin

2 cl white rum

2 cl red vermouth (Vermouth Rosso)

2 cl orange juice (preferably freshly squeezed)

Ice cube

You will also need a shaker. A sieve is also necessary.

Preparation:

1. put all the ingredients in the shaker with the ice cubes and shake vigorously.

2. then pour through a sieve into a fresh glass.

3. you can use an orange slice for decoration.

FLYING

The Flying is not to be confused with the following and probably better known Flying Dutchman, but is its own mix.

Ingredients for 1 jar:

2 cl gin

1 cl Triple Sec

1 cl lemon juice (preferably freshly squeezed)

Approx. 7 cl sparkling wine (to top up)

Ice cube

You will also need a shaker. A sieve is also necessary.

Preparation:

Put the gin, triple sec and lemon juice into a shaker with ice cubes and shake.

Pour the mixture through the sieve into a fresh glass.

Top up with sparkling wine.

FLYING DUTCHMAN

Flying Dutchman is a household name for most in many ways. There is also a drink with the name of the famous ghost ship.

Ingredients for 1 jar:

4 cl gin (preferably genever)

1 cl triple sec

1 cl Orange Bitters

1 lime

Ice cube

Preparation:

Put ice cubes in a glass and pour in all the liquid ingredients. This will cool the drink down faster.

2. stir.

Finally, cut the lime into eighths and squeeze a piece over the drink.

Decorate with another eighth.

FOG CUTTER

The Fog Cutter has a slightly tart taste and is easy to prepare. It is suitable for sociable informal evenings.

Ingredients for 1 jar:

15 ml gin

45 ml Rum Light

25 ml cognac

45 ml orange juice (preferably freshly squeezed)

15 ml lemon juice (preferably freshly squeezed)

15 ml Orgeat (almond syrup)

15 ml sherry

Ice cube

You will also need a shaker.

Preparation:

1. put all the ingredients in the shaker except the sherry.

Shake the mix and pour it into a glass.

Add the sherry.

Decorate with a piece of orange.

SAMOAN FOG CUTTER

The Samoan Fog Cutter also tastes slightly tart, but has a sour additive. It differs from the Fog Cutter in the quantities.

Ingredients for 1 jar:

2 cl gin

1 cl sherry

2 cl brandy

4 cl Rum Light

3 cl orange juice (preferably freshly squeezed)

6 cl lemon juice (preferably freshly squeezed)

1 cl Orgeat (almond syrup)

Crushed ice

Ice cube

You will also need a shaker.

Preparation:

1. put all the ingredients in the shaker except the sherry.

Shake the mix and pour it into a glass filled with ice cubes.

Add the sherry.

Decorate with a piece of orange. Alternatively, a sprig of mint is also suitable.

FRANCIS

Tart yet sweet: this is probably the best way to describe Francis.

Ingredients for 1 jar:

3 cl gin

4 cl Aperol

3 cl grapefruit juice

10 cl bitter lemon

Ice cube

You also need a shaker. Furthermore, a sieve is necessary.

Preparation:

Put everything except the bitter lemon in the shaker and shake.

Pour over the sieve into a glass filled with ice cubes and top up with bitter lemon.

FRENCH 75

The French 75 is a fine drop due to the addition of champagne.

Ingredients for 1 jar:

3 cl gin

2cl lemon juice (preferably freshly squeezed)

1 cl Triple Sec

10 cl champagne

Furthermore, a shaker is necessary.

Preparation:

1. chill a glass before preparation.

2. put everything except the champagne in the shaker and shake it.

Pour the mixture into the cold glass and add the champagne.

GENOVA

The Genova is a simple drink with a special touch.

Ingredients for 1 jar:

4 cl gin

3 cl grappa

1 cl Sambuca

1 cl dry vermouth (Vermouth Dry)

Ice cube

You will also need a sieve.

Preparation:

1. chill a glass before preparation.

2. put all the ingredients in a jar and stir thoroughly.

Pour the mixture through a sieve into the chilled glass.

Serve immediately and enjoy.

GIMLET

The gimlet is a classic drink with gin that tastes fruity and is quick to prepare. Are you expecting spontaneous visitors? Then it's perfect.

Ingredients for 1 jar:

6 cl gin

2 cl Lime Juice (lime syrup)

1 lime

Ice cube

You will also need a shaker. You will also need a sieve.

Preparation:

1. chill a glass before preparation.

Add the gin, lime juice and the juice of a quartered lime to the shaker over ice cubes and shake the mixture.

3. pour through a sieve into the chilled glass.

Decorate with lime slices.

GINGERBALL

There are two official variants of the Gingerball. One with whiskey and one with gin, which I present to you here.

Ingredients for 1 jar:

2 cl gin

3 cl Bénédictine

2 cl pineapple juice (preferably freshly squeezed)

12 cl ginger ale

Ice cubes.

You will also need a shaker.

Preparation:

Add the gin, Bénédictine and pineapple juice to the shaker over ice cubes and shake.

Pour into a glass.

Fill up with ginger ale.

GREEN 43

You probably know the drink 43 Milk. However, you can also mix the liqueur very well with gin, which I present to you here.

Ingredients for 1 jar:

2 cl gin

2 cl Blue Curacao

2 cl Licor 43

1 cl lime juice (preferably freshly squeezed)

10 cl passion fruit juice (preferably freshly squeezed)

Ice cube

A shaker is also needed.

Preparation:

The preparation is extremely simple. Put everything in the shaker and shake it, then pour the drink into a glass.

Hint:

Kiwi slices are suitable for decoration.

GREEN JADE

The Green Jade is not to be confused with the Jade. There is no gin in the latter and the other ingredients are also different.

Ingredients for 1 jar:

3 cl gin

2 cl peppermint liqueur

6 cl cream

Ice cube

A shaker is also needed

Preparation:

To prepare, put everything together in the shaker, shake and serve the drink in a glass.

GREEN MORNING

The Green Morning is, even if it sounds like it, not a breakfast drink. At least not necessarily. On holiday, you can certainly enjoy this cocktail in the morning hours.

Ingredients for 1 jar:

4 cl gin

2 cl Blue Curacao

4 cl pineapple juice (preferably freshly squeezed)

4 cl orange juice (preferably freshly squeezed)

4 cl grapefruit juice (preferably freshly squeezed)

Ice cubes.

You will also need a shaker.

Preparation:

1. put all the ingredients in the shaker and shake it.

Fill a glass with ice cubes.

Pour the mixture over the ice cubes. This will cool the drink down faster.

HAWAIIAN VARIANT 1

The Hawaiian is a medium sweet drink of which there are two variants. I present both of them to you.

Ingredients for 1 jar:

4 cl gin

2 cl Orange Curacao

2 cl pineapple juice (preferably freshly squeezed)

Ice cube

You also need a shaker. Also a sieve.

Preparation:

1. put all the ingredients in the shaker and shake it until some foam forms.

Pour the mixture through the sieve into a glass.

3. you can use a pineapple slice for decoration.

HAWAIIAN COCKTAIL (OR: VARIATION 2)

The Hawaiian Cocktail is the second variation of the drink. Sometimes it actually has the addition "cocktail", which makes a distinction possible.

Ingredients for 1 jar:

2 cl gin

2 cl orange juice (preferably freshly squeezed)

1 cl Triple Sec

Ice cube

You also need a shaker. Also a (bar) strainer.

Preparation:

1. put all the ingredients in the shaker and shake it until some foam forms.

Pour the mixture through the sieve into a glass.

3. you can use an orange slice for decoration.

HELICOPTER

There are also different variants for the helicopter. Of course, you can vary according to your taste and preferences. I'll give you my favourite variant of the helicopter here, which is also a more familiar one.

Ingredients for 1 jar:

4 cl gin

4 cl tequila

2 cl Triple Sec

2 cl lime syrup

Tonic Water

Ice cube

You will also need a shaker

Preparation:

Mix all ingredients except tonic water in a blender.

Pour the mix into a fresh glass.

Finally, top up the drink with tonic water.

HENDERSON PRIME

The Henderson Prime, as the name suggests, is made with Henderson Gin.

Ingredients for 1 jar:

4 cl gin (Henderson London Dry Gin)

4 cl pink grapefruit (freshly squeezed)

2 cl lime syrup

Ice cube

Preparation:

The preparation is extremely simple. Put everything in a glass and stir the drink.

Hint:

If you prefer lime juice, you can also squeeze limes.

HOLY BARTENDER

The Holy Bartender should attain a dark blue to purple colour after preparation.

Ingredients for 1 jar:

2 cl gin

4 cl tequila

2 cl Triple Sec

2 cl Blue Curacao

1 cl grenadine

1 cl sugar syrup

Bitter Lemon

Ice cube

You will also need a shaker. You will also need a sieve.

Preparation:

Add everything except the bitter lemon to the shaker and shake.

Drain the mix through a sieve into a glass filled with fresh ice cubes. This will cool the drink more quickly.

Fill up the cocktail with bitter lemon.

JACK COUSTEAU

The Jack Cousteau cocktail was named after the famous ocean explorer.

Ingredients for 1 jar:

2 cl gin

2cl vodka

2 cl Blue Curacao

2 cl tonic water

Ice cube

Preparation:

The preparation is extremely simple. Put everything in a glass and stir the drink.

JOY OF LOVE

The Joy of Love is a fresh fruity tasting cocktail.

Ingredients for 1 jar:

4 cl gin

2 cl Apricot Brandy

2 cl lime juice (preferably freshly squeezed)

1 cl grenadine

12 cl passion fruit juice (preferably freshly squeezed)

Crushed ice

You will also need a shaker

Preparation:

1. add all the ingredients together in the shaker and shake it well.

Pour the mixture into a glass.

Hint:

Lime wedges are suitable for decoration. You can also use a cocktail cherry.

KNOCK OUT

The Knock Out sounds like a strong drink, but it is rather moderate.

Ingredients for 1 jar:

2 cl gin

1 cl Crème de Menthe (peppermint liqueur)

2 cl dry vermouth (Vermouth Dry)

2 cl Anisée (Pernod)

Ice cube

Preparation:

1. add all the ingredients together in the shaker and shake it well.

Pour the mixture into a glass.

Hint:

A sprig of mint is suitable for decoration. You can also use a cocktail cherry.

LADY KILLER

The Lady Killer is on many drink menus. However, many young adults would probably not describe it as a real "killer" in the form of a strong effect. They like to drink it especially if they like a fruity mixture that reminds them of summer evenings.

Ingredients for 1 jar:

3 cl gin

2 cl orange liqueur (Cointreau)

2 cl Apricot Brandy

5 cl pineapple juice (preferably freshly squeezed)

5 cl passion fruit juice (preferably freshly squeezed)

Ice cube

You will also need a shaker. You will also need a sieve.

Preparation:

1. chill a glass before starting.

Put all the ingredients in the shaker and shake well until it foams.

Pour the mixture through a sieve into the pre-chilled glass on fresh ice cubes. This cools the drink more quickly.

LADYLOVE

There are several variations of the LadyLove drink, as with all cocktails. I will of course present the one with gin.

Ingredients for 1 jar:

2 cl gin

4 cl Malibu

2 cl grenadine

1 cl lemon juice (preferably freshly squeezed)

6 cl orange juice (preferably freshly squeezed)

4 cl passion fruit juice (preferably freshly squeezed)

Ice cube

Furthermore, you need a shaker for mixing.

Preparation:

The preparation is extremely simple. Mix all the ingredients in a shaker and pour the result into a glass.

Hint:

Orange slices and a raspberry are suitable for decoration.

LAST WORD

The Last Word Cocktail is a traditional drink.

Ingredients for 1 jar:

2 cl gin

2 cl Green Chartreuse

2 cl maraschino

2cl lime juice (preferably freshly squeezed)

Ice cube

You will also need a shaker.

Preparation:

Mix all the ingredients together in the shaker and shake vigorously.

2. then put the mixture into a glass.

3. serve.

LIBERTINY

The Libertiny is a simple and flavourful drink at the same time.

Ingredients for 1 jar:

3 cl gin

3 cl Blue Curacao

2 cl lime juice (preferably freshly squeezed)

Ice cube

A shaker is also needed.

Preparation:

Put everything together in the shaker and pour it into a glass after shaking. Lime slices are suitable for decoration.

LIQUID FIRE

The Liquid Fire lives up to its name if you prepare it correctly. Mixing this drink should be a real eye-catcher.

Ingredients for 1 jar:

1 cl gin

1 cl brown rum

1cl tequila

1 cl vodka

3 cl Triple Sec

Preparation:

1. mix all the ingredients together in a glass and light it.

Pour the drink into a drinking glass while the flame is burning. But be careful: In order to make this an eye-catcher and for the "Liquid Fire" to come out properly, this should be done slowly while you pull up the glass from which you are pouring.

Hint:

After the controlled burn, you should not smell the drink. It smells nowhere near as good as it tastes.

LOCO KULAU

The Loco Kulau is a very interesting drink. Its appearance alone makes this clear; it's true: the eye drinks with the drink.

Ingredients for 1 jar:

2 cl gin

2 cl Triple Sec

2 cl Prosecco

2 cl ginger ale

2 cl mango syrup

1 cl strawberry syrup

Juice of half a lemon

1 coconut

Ice cube

You will also need a shaker.

Preparation:

1. cover the coconut in such a way that one can drink from it.

Fill the empty coconut with ice cubes.

Fill the blender with all the ingredients except the ginger ale and the prosecco.

4. after shaking, pour the drink into the coconut over the ice cubes.

Top up with ginger ale and prosecco.

Hint:

A beautiful large flower is suitable for decoration.

LONDON FEVER

London Fever is a sweet but refreshing drink.

Ingredients for 1 jar:

3 cl gin

2 cl white rum

3 cl lemon juice or optionally lime juice (preferably freshly squeezed)

1 cl grenadine

Soda

Ice cube

You will also need a shaker. You will also need a sieve.

Preparation:

1. put everything except the soda in the shaker and shake.

2. pour the mixture through the sieve into a glass.

Fill up with soda.

Hint:

Make sure that the soda for this cocktail is quite cold. As the drink is served without ice cubes, it is advantageous to use ice-cold soda.

LOUISIANA

The Louisiana is a tart short drink and should not be confused with the Louisiana Sour, which is prepared without gin.

Ingredients for 1 jar:

2 cl gin

2 cl Apricot Brandy

2 cl grapefruit juice (preferably freshly squeezed)

Ice cube

You will also need a shaker. You will also need a sieve.

Preparation:

Add all ingredients to the shaker and shake vigorously.

Pour over the sieve into a glass.

3. enjoy.

Hint:

You can shorten or double the mixture, the important thing here is that all ingredients are used in equal parts.

LUCKY GRIZZLY

The Lucky Grizzly in with many juices is a fruity cocktail, which however does not taste too sweet.

Ingredients for 1 jar:

2 cl gin

2 cl peach liqueur

1 cl grenadine

6 cl passion fruit nectar (preferably freshly squeezed)

4 cl grapefruit juice (preferably freshly squeezed)

Ice cube

You will also need a shaker. You will also need a sieve.

Preparation:

1. put all the ingredients in the shaker and shake it.

Pour the mixture through a sieve into a fresh glass with ice cubes. This will cool the drink more quickly.

Decorate the drink with a little grapefruit.

MANHATTAN (NO. 2)

The Manhattan No. 2 is not to be compared with the Manhattan. In fact, the official name of the cocktail with gin has the addition No. 2.

Ingredients for 1 jar:

4 cl gin

2 cl red vermouth (Vermouth Rosso)

1 cl Angostura bitters

Ice cube

Preparation:

The preparation is extremely simple. Put all the ingredients in a glass and stir before serving.

MILKY WAY

When they think of Milky Way, many people think first of the chocolate bar, then of the Milky Way. But there is also a cocktail that bears this name.

Ingredients for 1 jar:

3 cl gin

3 cl amaretto

2 cl strawberry syrup

6 cl pineapple juice (preferably freshly squeezed)

Ice cube

You will also need a shaker. You will also need a sieve.

Preparation:

1. put all the ingredients in the shaker and shake it.

Pour the mixture through a sieve into a fresh glass with ice cubes. This will cool the drink more quickly.

MILLION DOLLAR COCKTAIL

The Million Dollar Cocktail is a noble drink to be served after dinner.

Ingredients for 1 jar:

4 cl gin

2 cl red vermouth (Vermouth Rosso)

2 cl pineapple juice (preferably freshly squeezed)

1 cl grenadine

Optional egg white of an egg

Ice cube

A shaker is also required.

Preparation:

1. chill a glass in advance.

Put all the ingredients in the shaker and shake.

Pour the mixture into the cold glass.

MINDLOVE

The Mindlove is made with cream and decorated with strawberries.

Ingredients for 1 jar:

4 cl gin

2 cl Prosecco

10 cl orange juice (preferably freshly squeezed)

2 cl cream

2 cl passion fruit juice (preferably freshly squeezed)

A shaker is also necessary.

Preparation:

1. chill a glass in advance.

Put all the ingredients in the shaker and shake.

Pour the mixture into the cold glass.

MOIDEL`S FLASH

The Moidel`s Flash has it all. It is a great cocktail and tastes great.

Ingredients for 1 (very large) jar:

2 cl gin

2 cl white rum

2 cl vodka

2 cl peach liqueur

Up to 2 cl coconut syrup

10 cl pineapple juice (preferably freshly squeezed)

2 cl Lime Juice

2 cl Lemon Squash

10 cl passion fruit nectar (preferably freshly squeezed)

Ice cubes and crushed ice

You will also need a shaker. You will also need a sieve.

Preparation:

1. put all the ingredients in the shaker with the ice cubes and shake the mixture.

Fill a glass with crushed ice.

Pour the drink through the strainer into the glass filled with crushed ice. This will cool the drink down more quickly.

Hint:

A pineapple slice is suitable for decoration.

NEGRONI

The Negroni is an Italian aperitif and simple to prepare.

Ingredients for 1 jar:

3 cl gin

3 cl Campari

3 cl red vermouth (Vermouth Rosso)

Ice cube

Preparation:

Pour everything into a glass and stir well once.

Hint:

If you want decoration, a slice of orange is suitable.

ORANGE BLOSSOM

The Orange Blossom is bursting with orange flavour.

Ingredients for 1 jar:

4 cl gin

4 cl orange juice (preferably freshly squeezed)

Ice cube

Preparation:

The preparation is extremely simple. Put both drinks in a glass with ice cubes and stir. This will cool the drink down faster.

A slice of orange is suitable for decoration.

Hint:

Actually, the Orange Blossom is mixed with a 1 to 1 mixture. If you don't like this, you can of course use more orange juice.

OUZO LAIKADA

The Ouzo Laikada is, as the name suggests, made with ouzo. This cocktail is something for gourmets.

Ingredients for 1 jar:

2 cl gin

2 cl ouzo

2 cl Crème de Bananes

1 cl passion fruit syrup

8 cl orange juice (preferably freshly squeezed)

Ice cube

You will also need a shaker. You will also need a sieve.

Preparation:

1. put all the ingredients in the shaker and shake it.

Pour the mixture through a sieve into a fresh glass.

Hint:

You can of course use orange slices for decoration, but banana pieces are also very popular.

PARADISE

The Paradise is a fruity cocktail, but it has it all. The preparation is quick.

Ingredients for 1 jar:

4 cl gin

2 cl Apricot Brandy

4 cl orange juice (preferably freshly squeezed)

Ice cube

You will also need a shaker.

Preparation:

To finish, put everything in the shaker, shake it and transfer the drink into a glass.

Hint:

Orange slices are suitable for decoration.

PINK BUBBLES

The name Pink Bubbles says it all.

Ingredients for 1 jar:

4 cl gin

4 cl Triple Sec

3 cl sugar syrup

3 cl grenadine

2 cl lime juice (preferably freshly squeezed)

2 cl lemon juice (preferably freshly squeezed)

15 cl pineapple juice (preferably freshly squeezed)

Ice cube

A shaker is also required.

Preparation:

1. put all the ingredients in the shaker and shake it.

Pour the mixture into a fresh glass.

Hint:

Since "little coward" is also available in bubble gum flavour, there is also a Pink Bubbles with this very drink. However, this is not to be compared with the Pink Bubbles with gin.

PINK GIN CHAMPAGNE

The Pink Gin Champagne is prepared with the Pink Gin. It is a modern gin, mainly aimed at women, which is slowly conquering the supermarkets. Of course, it can also be consumed by men.

Ingredients for 1 jar:

4 cl Pink Gin

Champagne

1 cl strawberry syrup

Ice cube

Strawberries

Preparation:

The preparation of the Pink Gin Champagne could not be easier.

Put ice cubes in a glass and add the Pink Gin. This will cool the drink down faster.

2. add the syrup and stir.

Fill up the glass with champagne.

Decorate with the strawberries.

Hint:

The strawberries and the syrup can be changed according to choice. Just make sure that you use sweet fruits. For example, raspberries.

PINK GIN STRAWBERRY CRUSH

The Pink Gin Strawberry Crush is suitable for summer party nights.

Ingredients for 1 jar:

3 cl Pink Gin

3 cl lime juice (preferably freshly squeezed)

2 cl strawberry syrup

150 ml soda

4 strawberries

Crushed ice

You will also need a blender.

Preparation:

Wash the strawberries and chop them up.

Purée the strawberries with the crushed ice, lime juice and syrup.

3. add the pink gin.

Pour the mixture into a glass and add soda.

PINK GIN SPRITZ

The Pink Gin Spritz is the last recipe in this book that is tailored to the Pink Gin. Its colour is not pink, but it still tastes sweet and exotic.

Ingredients for 1 jar:

4 cl Pink Gin

1 cl Aperol

Prosecco

Fruit of your choice

Ice cube

Preparation:

Put the ice cubes and the fruit in a glass.

Add Pink Gin and Aperol. This will cool the drink down faster.

Top up with Prosecco and stir briefly.

Hint:

The fruits you have chosen are suitable for decoration. Or fresh mint.

PINK LADY

The Pink Lady is one thing above all: Pink!

Ingredients for 1 jar:

4 cl gin

2 cl Cointreau

1 cl grenadine

1 cl lemon juice (preferably freshly squeezed)

Ice cube

You will also need a shaker. You will also need a sieve.

Preparation:

1. put all the ingredients in the shaker and shake it.

Pour the mixture through a sieve into a fresh glass.

Hint:

If you would rather have the pink drink in a soft pink, there is another variation. Add one egg white of an ice cream and a little icing sugar to the shaker. Voila, you have a different drink.

PINK ROSE

The Pink Rose is very similar to the Pink Lady in its variation with the egg white. However, there is another subtle difference.

Ingredients for 1 jar:

5 cl gin

1 cl grenadine

1 cl lemon juice (preferably freshly squeezed)

2 cl cream

1 egg white

Ice cube

You will also need a shaker. You will also need a sieve.

Preparation:

1. put all the ingredients in the shaker and shake it.

Pour the mixture through a sieve into a fresh glass.

PURPLE HAZE

The Purple Haze offers a purple look for a change. Moreover, the preparation is very easy.

Ingredients for 1 jar:

4 cl gin

2 cl Blue Curacao

2 cl grenadine

Tonic Water

Crushed ice

Preparation:

1. put everything except the tonic water in the shaker.

2. shake, shake, shake.

Fill the mixture into a glass and top up with tonic water.

RED GIN

The Red Gin tastes rather sweet and convinces with a cherry note.

Ingredients for 1 jar:

3 cl gin

2 cl cherry liqueur

1 cl lime juice (preferably freshly squeezed)

You will also need a shaker.

Preparation:

1. before mixing, chill a glass until it is really icy (not frozen).

Shake the ingredients in the shaker.

3. then pour into the cold glass.

Hint:

Cherries or optionally a slice of lime are suitable for decoration.

RED HOURS

At Red Hours you see red.

Ingredients for 1 jar:

2 cl gin

2 cl red vermouth (Vermouth Rosso)

5 cl grape juice (preferably red)

1 cl lime juice (preferably freshly squeezed)

Sugar

Ice cube

You will also need a shaker.

Preparation:

Before you start, dip the glass in which you want to serve the cocktail in the lime juice. Then dab it in the sugar to create a sugar rim.

Shake the gin, vermouth and grape juice in a shaker.

Then pour into the glass with the sugar rim.

4. finally, add a few squirts of lime juice.

RED PASSION

There are several Red Passion recipes. Why? Because each one is unique on its own. If you look closely at these recipes, you will quickly notice that they have nothing in common, however, because the ingredients are different depending on the addition of alcohol.

Ingredients for 1 jar:

3 cl Dry Gin

20 cl cranberry juice

Fresh basil leaves

Ice cube

You will also need a shaker.

Preparation:

First, put the basil leaves in the shaker and crush them.

Then add the rest of the ingredients to the shaker and shake vigorously.

Pour the mixture into a drinking glass.

Decorate with basil. Optional cranberries.

Hint:

If you don't like the aroma of basil, you can leave it out. Even without the addition, it is still an original Red Passion.

RED SNAPPER

The Red Snapper is, so to speak, the Bloody Mary among gin drinks.

Ingredients for 1 jar:

5 cl gin

12 cl tomato juice

1 cl lemon juice (preferably freshly squeezed)

1 cl Worcester sauce

Dash of Tabasco

Pepper and salt

Ice cube

Preparation:

1. put all the liquid ingredients except the tomato juice in a glass and stir everything together.

Top up with tomato juice.

Season to taste.

Stir again and serve.

SILVER JUBILEE

The Silver Jubilee is a creamy cocktail that is easy to prepare.

Ingredients for 1 jar:

3 cl gin

3 cl banana liqueur (Crème de Bananes)

4 cl cream

Ice cube

Furthermore, a shaker is needed. You will also need a (bar) strainer.

Preparation:

1. put all the ingredients in the shaker and shake it.

Pour the mixture through a sieve into a fresh glass.

Hint:

A piece of banana is suitable for decoration.

SUMMER COOLER

The Summer Cooler is a refreshing drink reminiscent of summer nights.

Ingredients for 1 jar:

4 cl gin

1 cl almond syrup

14 cl orange juice (preferably freshly squeezed)

2 cl lemon juice (preferably freshly squeezed)

Ice cube

A shaker is also needed.

Preparation:

Add the liquid ingredients to the shaker and shake.

Put the ice cubes in a glass (approx. 4 pieces).

Pour the mixed drink over the ice cubes in the glass. This will cool the drink down faster.

SWEET DREAM

The Sweet Dream is, contrary to its name, not sweet, but rather fine tart.

Ingredients for 1 jar:

2 cl gin

6 cl champagne

1 cl Grand Marnier

1 cl crème de cassis

1 cl lemon juice (preferably freshly squeezed)

1 cl orange juice (preferably freshly squeezed)

You will also need a shaker.

Preparation:

1. chill the glass in which you want to serve the drink in advance.

Mix all the alcoholic ingredients together in a shaker.

Fill the mix into the cold glass and add the juices at the end.

Hint:

It is also possible to mix the drink with crushed ice. Then you still need a (bar) strainer to filter out the ice cubes after shaking.

TANGO

There are many different recipes for the Tango. Most have different bases, which is why I present the recipe with gin here.

Ingredients for 1 jar:

2 cl gin

2 cl red vermouth (Vermouth Rosso)

2 cl Cointreau

8 cl orange juice (preferably freshly squeezed)

2 cl lemon juice (preferably freshly squeezed)

Ice cubes and crushed ice

You will also need a shaker. You will also need a sieve.

Preparation:

1. put all the ingredients in the shaker and shake it.

Pour the mixture through a sieve into a glass filled with crushed ice. This will cool the drink down more quickly.

Hint:

Orange or lemon slices are suitable for decoration. Furthermore, you can work with cocktail cherries.

TOM COLLINS

The Tom Collins is a classic, like the Gin Fizz or the Gin Sour. They are all a little similar, with the Tom Collins being closer to the Gin Fizz. One important difference, however, is that the Tom Collins is stirred.

Ingredients for 1 jar:

5 cl gin (Old Tom Gin)

2 cl sugar syrup

3 cl lemon juice (preferably freshly squeezed)

Soda

Ice cube

Preparation:

1. although with most drinks you put the ice cubes in the glass first, with the Tom Collins it is done differently. First put the gin, syrup and lemon juice in a glass.

2. stir.

Now add ice cubes to taste.

Fill up with the soda (preferably cold).

Hint:

The Tom Collins is only an original when it is prepared with the Old Tom Gin.

In addition to a slice of lemon, a cocktail cherry is suitable for decoration.

TROPIC BITTER

Tropic Bitter is, as the name suggests, a bitter drink.

Ingredients for 1 jar:

2 cl gin

2 cl Cinzano Bitter (optionally Campari Bitter)

2 cl Cointreau

4 cl orange juice (preferably freshly squeezed)

10 cl Bitter Lemon (optionally Orange Bitter)

Ice cube

You will also need a shaker. You will also need a sieve.

Preparation:

Put all the ingredients except the bitter lemon (or orange bitters) in the shaker and shake vigorously.

Pour into a glass through a sieve.

Top up with Bitter Lemon (or Orange Bitter).

Hint:

You can also prepare this drink without a shaker and strainer. Here we recommend filling the glass as much as possible with ice cubes and stirring the mixture vigorously.

TROPIC CAMPARI

Tropic Campari is similar to Tropic Bitter, but differs mainly in one ingredient.

Ingredients for 1 jar:

2 cl gin

3 cl Campari Bitter

2 cl Grand Marnier

4 cl orange juice (preferably freshly squeezed)

15 cl Orange Bitter (optionally Bitter Lemon)

Ice cube

Furthermore, a shaker is necessary.

Preparation:

Add all ingredients except Orange Bitter (or Bitter Lemon) to the shaker and shake.

Pour into a glass.

Top up with Orange Bitter (or Bitter Lemon).

Hint:

In Tropic Campari, Campari Bitter is a basic ingredient that should not be substituted.

TROPICAL RED

The Tropical Red is easy to prepare, but don't be surprised by the colour: the drink looks rather orange.

Ingredients for 1 jar:

2 cl gin

3 cl orange liqueur

6 cl orange juice (preferably freshly squeezed)

6 cl grapefruit juice (preferably freshly squeezed)

Ice cube

You will also need a shaker. You will also need a sieve.

Preparation:

1. put all the ingredients in the shaker and shake it.

Pour the mixture through a sieve into a glass.

TROPICAL DERBY

The Tropical Derby looks exotic and will remind you of tropical nights.

Ingredients for 1 jar:

6 cl gin

2 cl grenadine

8 cl orange juice (preferably freshly squeezed)

8 cl passion fruit juice (preferably freshly squeezed)

8 cl pineapple juice (preferably freshly squeezed)

1 cl lemon juice (preferably freshly squeezed)

Ice cube

You will also need a shaker. You will also need a sieve.

Preparation:

1. put all the ingredients in the shaker and shake it.

Pour the mixture through a sieve into a glass filled with fresh ice cubes. This cools the drink more quickly.

Hint:

A slice of orange is suitable for decoration.

TROUBLEMAKER

The Troublemaker does not necessarily live up to its name. It is a delicious cocktail that is also easy to prepare. But if you're expecting a quick buzz, you're thinking wrong.

Ingredients for 1 jar:

4 cl gin

2 cl Apricot Brandy

1 cl lemon juice (preferably freshly squeezed)

1 cl grenadine

Ice cube

You will also need a shaker. You will also need a sieve.

Preparation:

1. put all the ingredients in the shaker and shake it.

Pour the mixture through a sieve into a glass filled with fresh ice cubes. This cools the drink more quickly.

Hint:

A slice of lemon is suitable for decoration.

VAMPIRE VARIANT 1

Once again, there are many recipes for the vampire. I will show you two here. First a very simple one and then my favourite recipe. Variant 1 is a sour form of the vampire.

Ingredients for 1 jar:

3 cl gin

3 cl dry vermouth (Vermouth Dry)

2 cl lime juice (preferably freshly squeezed)

A shaker is also necessary.

Preparation:

1. chill the glass in which you want to serve the drink in advance.

Mix the gin and vermouth in a shaker.

Pour the mixture into the cold glass and add the lime juice.

Note:
No decoration is used here.

VAMPIRE VARIANT 2

This recipe is one of my favourites. Especially for theme parties and Halloween, this drink will be a real eye-catcher.

Ingredients for 1 jar:

2 cl gin

2 cl vodka

3 cl rum (preferably white rum)

4 cl cream

2 cl almond syrup

6 cl pineapple juice (preferably freshly squeezed)

1 cl passion fruit juice (preferably freshly squeezed)

1 cl grenadine

Crushed ice

Ice cube

You will also need a shaker.

Preparation:

Fill the shaker with ice cubes and all liquid ingredients except grenadine.

Add crushed ice to the empty glass and pour in the mix from the shaker.

3. at the end, pour the grenadine slowly and preferably along the rim so that the liquid runs along the rim (inside) of the glass to the bottom.

Hint:

If the drink is too watery for you, you can dispense with the crushed ice.

VANITY

The vanity makes a beautiful picture if you decorate it with a physalis at the end.

Ingredients for 1 jar:

2 cl gin

2 cl Blue Curacao

1 cl grenadine

2 cl lemon juice (preferably freshly squeezed)

3 cl pineapple juice (preferably freshly squeezed)

Ice cube

You will also need a shaker.

Preparation:

The preparation is extremely simple. Put all the ingredients together in the shaker, shake it and pour everything into a glass at the end.

WAIKIKI BEACHCOMBER

The Waikiki Beachcomber is described as a strong drink. It is also based on the Martini.

Ingredients for 1 jar:

3 cl gin

2 cl Cointreau

1 cl pineapple juice (preferably freshly squeezed)

You will also need a shaker. You will also need a sieve.

Preparation:

1. chill a glass before mixing.

Put all the ingredients in the shaker and shake.

Pour the mixture through a sieve into the chilled glass.

WELCOME STRANGER

The Welcome Stranger - or simply Welcome - impresses with its medium sweet taste.

Ingredients for 1 jar:

2 cl gin

2 cl brandy

2 cl grenadine

2 cl orange juice (preferably freshly squeezed)

2 cl lemon juice (preferably freshly squeezed)

Ice cube

A shaker is also needed.

Preparation:

Add all the ingredients to the shaker and shake.

After shaking, pour everything into a glass.

Hint:

Especially for the Christmas season, the addition of 1 to 2 cl of Swedish punch is recommended.

WET MARTINA

With the Wet Martina Drink, it is also important to add the right amount. Here you should rely on your taste.

Ingredients for 1 jar:

4 cl gin

2 cl Martini Bianco

6 cl pineapple juice (preferably freshly squeezed)

Ice cube

A shaker is also required.

Preparation:

The preparation is very simple.

Put everything in the shaker and, after shaking, pour the drink into a glass.

Hint:

As mentioned above, it strongly depends on the amount of alcoholic liquids. You should not give up if you do not like the drink after the first time. Feel free to try a 1 to 1 mixture.

WHITE LADY

The White Lady Cocktail is a real Frenchman and certainly not just for the ladies.

Ingredients for 1 jar:

2 cl gin

2 cl Cointreau

2 cl lemon juice (preferably freshly squeezed)

Ice cube

A shaker is also needed.

Preparation:

Add all the ingredients to the shaker and shake.

2. after mixing, transfer everything into a glass.

Hint:

To give the drink a little more flair, you can add egg whites of an ice cream.

Cocktails without alcohol

DELICIOUS IPANEMA

Ingredients for 4 glasses:

2 untreated limes
4 tbsp. cane sugar
8 cl passion fruit juice
24 cl ginger ale
Crushed ice

Preparation:

First, wash the lime, then dry it and then cut it into fine slices.

Now distribute the columns in the glasses and mash them a little so that fresh juice forms.

Put about a tablespoon of sugar in each glass, then mix the two together.

Fill the glasses with crushed ice and add 2 cl passion fruit juice to each. Then stir well.

Finally, fill the glasses with ginger ale. Garnish the cocktails as desired and serve immediately.

FRUITY VIRGIN SUNRISE

Ingredients for 4 glasses:

300 ml orange juice
170 ml pineapple juice
4 tsp fresh lemon juice
40 ml grenadine
a few ice cubes

Preparation:

Take a cocktail shaker or another mixer and pour the three juices into it. Then fill the ice cubes into the glasses.

Then pour the juice mixture into the glasses.

Then slowly spoon the grenadine around the rim of the glasses to create the colours of the cocktail.

Garnish with fresh pineapple or oranges as desired and enjoy.

COLOURFUL RAINBOW COCKTAIL

Ingredients for 2 glasses:

200 ml cold mineral water with plenty of carbonic acid
1 pinch blue food colouring
400 ml orange-mango juice
60 ml grenadine
2 skewers
Gummi bears to taste

Preparation:

In the first step, colour the mineral water with the food colouring.

First, pour the orange-mango juice into two cocktail glasses.

Then add the grenadine via a teaspoon at the edge of the glass with feeling. Then different colours appear in the cocktail - like a rainbow.

Now pour the blue water into the glass in the same way with a teaspoon so that the colour changes once again.

Then put the gummy bears on the skewers as you like and decorate the jar with creativity.

REFRESHING NOJITO (MOJITO WITHOUT ALCOHOL)

Ingredients for 4 glasses:

1 bunch fresh mint
2 untreated limes
4 tbsp brown sugar
Crushed ice
500 ml ginger ale

Preparation:

Wash the mint and the limes. Then dry them and pluck the mint leaves from the stems. Cut the limes into wedges.

Distribute the mint evenly among the glasses and crush them a little. Then add the limes and crush them as well.

Then pour a tablespoon of brown sugar into each of the glasses and then top up with ginger ale. Garnish the glasses with fresh mint and serve immediately.

SPARKLING MOJITO WITH FRESH MANGO

Ingredients for 2 glasses:

1 ripe mango
1 fresh lime
1 half bunch fresh mint
0.5 l cold mineral water
a few ice cubes

Preparation:

First, peel the ripe mango and carefully cut the flesh from the core.

Then halve the lime and squeeze out the fresh juice.

Then finely puree the flesh of the mango, the juice of the lime and about 12 leaves of mint with a stand mixer - you can also use a stick.

Now divide the mixture between two glasses and pour about 200 ml of cold mineral water into each.

Finally, add a few ice cubes to each glass. Garnish the cocktails with a fresh sprig of mint if desired.

INVIGORATING HUGO

Ingredients for 4 glasses:

350 ml ginger ale
70 ml elderflower syrup
Juice of two limes
1 organic lime
1 organic lemon
3 fresh sprigs of mint
400 ml cold mineral water
a few ice cubes

Preparation:

First, mix the ginger ale, syrup, and fresh lime juice. Then add the fresh sprigs of mint and top up with the cold mineral water.

Now wash the organic lime in hot water and pat dry. Now slice it and cut it in half. Leave four slices and add the other slices to the remaining ingredients.

Fill four large glasses halfway with ice cubes or crushed ice and pour the non-alcoholic Hugo into the glasses. Garnish each glass with a slice of lime.

DELICIOUS TONIC WITH CHERRY AND APPLE

Ingredients for 1 jar:
100 ml tonic water
50 ml apple juice
100 ml sour cherry nectar
1 squeeze of fresh lime
2 fresh sprigs of mint

Preparation:
In the first step, fill a shaker with the cherry nectar. Add a few ice cubes and crush the mint. Now shake the whole thing vigorously for about 10 seconds.

Now pour the contents of the shaker through a sieve into a suitable glass. Then fill the glass with tonic water and apple juice. Then add fresh squirts of lime juice if desired.

Some fresh mint can be used for decoration.

AUTUMN ROSEHIP COCKTAIL

Ingredients for 4 glasses:

4 bags rose hip tea
2 tbsp. vanilla syrup
2 tbsp hazelnut syrup
4 tsp lemon juice
60 cl ginger ale
4 vanilla beans

Preparation:

First, boil 400 ml in a kettle and then pour it over the tea bags. Let it steep for about 7 minutes. Then remove the tea bags and let the tea cool.

Then mix the vanilla syrup with the hazelnut syrup. Add the lemon juice and the tea.

It is best to use larger glasses (about 0.3 l). Then fill them with ice cubes and pour the finished cocktail evenly into them. Top up each glass with some ginger ale.

Decorate the cocktail with whole vanilla beans.

TROPICAL COCKTAIL WITH FRESH PINEAPPLE

Ingredients for 2 glasses:

1 pineapple
3 stalks fresh mint
200 ml fresh or bought orange juice
400 ml mango-passion fruit juice
200 ml pineapple juice

Preparation:

First, cut off the ends of the pineapple. Then peel and cut into quarters. Remove the stalk of the fruit and cut it into small pieces.

Now wash the mint, dab dry and put the leaves on skewers together with the pineapple.

Mix the juices together and fill the glasses with ice cubes. Decorate the finished cocktail with pineapple-mint skewers.

DELICIOUS SAN FRANCISCO

Ingredients for 1 jar:

7 cl pineapple juice
2 cl grenadine
7 cl passion fruit juice
1 squeeze of fresh orange juice
3 cl lemon juice
Ice cream

Preparation:

Fill a shaker with the lemon juice, orange juice and passion fruit juice. Add ice cubes or crushed ice and shake thoroughly.

Fill a large cocktail glass with ice and pour the cocktail over it.

Then pour in the grenadine to create a beautiful colour.

Attach an orange slice to the rim of the glass for decoration and enjoy the San Francisco immediately.

WOODRUFF COCKTAIL FOR CHILDREN

Ingredients for 4 glasses:

4 tbsp woodruff syrup
0.8 l cold mineral water
0.8 l cold apple juice
some crushed ice
Effervescent powder in different colours

Preparation:

Fill a large bottle with mineral water and then add the syrup.

Then fill a saucer with water and put the different sherbet powder on other saucers.

Now hold the rims of the glasses in the water and then press them into the different colours to create a beautiful rim.

Then fill the glasses halfway with crushed ice. Now pour 150 ml apple juice over it and top up with the woodruff mineral water mixture. Serve the cocktails with colourful straws.

FRUITY MULTI COLADA

Ingredients for 2 - 4 glasses:

1 pomegranate
3 untreated limes
1 baby pineapple
750 ml vitamin juice
160 ml coconut milk

Preparation:

First, halve the pomegranate and remove the seeds with a spoon.

Now wash a lime in hot water, let it dry and cut it into 8 slices.

Then peel the pineapple and cut it lengthwise into quarters. Make sure that you carefully cut through the leaves. Remove the stalk of the fruit.

Halve the remaining limes.

Now add the juice of one lime, the vitamin juice and the coconut milk to a shaker and mix thoroughly.

Then divide 4 tablespoons of pomegranate seeds and 4 lime slices between 2 glasses and top up with the drink. Depending on the size of the glasses, you can repeat this process with two more glasses.

Decorate the glasses with the sliced pineapple.

SWEET MANGO GINGER COCKTAIL

Ingredients for 6 glasses:

1 ripe mango
2 tbsp elderflower syrup
1 tablespoon sugar
5 cm ginger bulb
a few ice cubes
cold mineral water

Preparation:

In the first step, cut out small balls from the mango with a small spoon or a melon cutter.

Then peel the ginger and cut it into very fine strips.

Then fill approx. 1 l of water with the elderflower syrup and sugar into glasses.

Arrange the whole thing with the mango and ginger. Finally, top up the glasses with mineral water and ice cubes.

MANGO COCKTAIL WITH ELDERBERRY

Ingredients for 1 jar:

100 g mango puree
2 tbsp elderflower syrup
½ tsp cumin seeds
100 g sugar
50 ml apple cider vinegar
cold mineral water
a few ice cubes

Preparation:

Cut 100 g of mango from the fruit and put it in a blender or puree it with a stick.

Put the puree in a pot with the other ingredients, except the water and the ice cubes.

Bring to the boil and then simmer for about 10 minutes until the sugar has dissolved. The end result is a syrup.

Now mix about 2 - 3 tablespoons of syrup with the mineral water and the ice cubes.

COLOURED COCKTAIL WITH KIWI

Ingredients for 2 glasses:

2 fresh kiwis
3 tbsp. orange juice
3 tbsp instant oatmeal
2 fresh peaches
150 g cherries from the jar

Preparation:

First, peel the kiwis and cut them into small pieces. Then puree them together with orange juice and with 1 tbsp instant oat flakes. Then put the mixture into 2 large glasses.

Then skin the peaches and chop them up. Puree them with 1 tablespoon of oat flakes. Now pour the mixture onto the kiwi mixture.

First, mash the cherries with the oat flakes. Then add these to the peaches so that you end up with three beautiful layers. Serve immediately.

CHAI BUBBLE TEA LATTE

Ingredients for 1 jar:

2 packets chai tea
some cinnamon
a little almond syrup
 Soy milk
Tapioca beads

Preparation:

First, mix the soy milk with the chai tea.

Then add a little cinnamon and almond syrup.

Add the tapioca pearls and enjoy the drink.

BOOSTER COCKTAIL WITH ROSEHIP

Ingredients for 1 jar:

200 ml cooled rose hip tea
200 ml cherry juice
Juice of half a lemon
a little zest of an untreated lemon
1 tsp apple syrup

Preparation:

First, boil 200 ml of water and add a few rosehip-flavoured tea bags. Add the apple syrup already at this stage so that it dissolves well. Then let it steep and wait until the tea has cooled down.

Now put all the ingredients in a shaker and shake everything thoroughly.

Finally, fill the finished cocktail into glasses and decorate them with fresh fruit and add the ice cubes.

FRESH FITNESS PINA COLADA

Ingredients for 1 jar:

200 g pineapple (fresh or canned)
30 g protein powder in vanilla or coconut flavour
1 tsp honey
1 tablespoon grated coconut
200 ml coconut milk from Alpro
200 ml water
some ice if desired

Preparation:

First, put the coconut milk, water and honey in a blender. Then add the grated coconut, protein powder, and pineapple.

Put a few pieces of pineapple on a skewer for decoration and put it in a glass.

Then add the cocktail. Add a few more ice cubes if desired.

HIGH PROTEIN SMOOTHIE COCKTAIL

Ingredients for 2 glasses:

200 g fresh pineapple
150 g low fat curd
150 g yoghurt (0.1 % fat)
100 ml coconut milk light
10 g coconut flakes
1 fresh lemon
some ice to taste

Preparation:

In the first step, peel the pineapple and cut off approx. 200 g of it. Then cut it into small pieces.

Now put the pieces into a blender with a little juice from the lemon. Blend briefly and then add the other ingredients.

Pour the finished High Protein Smoothie Cocktail into two large glasses and add ice if desired.

DELICIOUS BERRY COCKTAIL

Ingredients for 4 glasses:

350 g berry mixture
1 Apple
1 pear
1 banana
0.8 l whey
80 g honey

Preparation:

First, wash all the berries. Then set aside some beautiful berries for decoration. Then put these berries on skewers and put them aside, covered.

Quarter the banana and also cut the apple and pear into smaller pieces.

Now put all the fruits into the blender. Then add the whey and the honey. Then pour the cocktail through a sieve into cocktail glasses.

Garnish with the berry skewers and serve with a straw.

BLUEBERRY BANANA COCKTAIL

Ingredients for 2 glasses:

2 very ripe bananas
350 g blueberries
20 cl milk
2 scoops vanilla ice cream
20 g brown sugar
a little fresh lemon juice

Preparation:

First, put all the ingredients, except for the ice into a blender, and puree everything finely.

Then pour the cocktail into two large glasses and add a scoop of ice to each.

Garnish the drinks with a few blueberries and serve with a spoon.

GREEN SMOOTHIE COCKTAIL

Ingredients for 1 jar:

1 cup spinach or kale (preferably frozen)
2 cups with different fruits
1 cup water
1 cup orange juice
1 cup almond milk
Spices such as cinnamon or turmeric to taste

Preparation:

It is best to use a stand mixer.

First, put the liquid ingredients into the blender and then the spinach and the various fruits.

Add spices to taste and then blend everything very finely.

Pour into a large glass and add a little ice if desired.

SIMPLE STRAWBERRY COCKTAIL

Ingredients for 1 jar:

Strawberries to taste
1 lemon
cold mineral water to top up
a few ice cubes

Preparation:

Squeeze half of the lemon and pour the juice directly into a glass.

Add a few ice cubes if desired.

Cut the rest of the lemon into small pieces and add them to the glass.

Now chop the strawberries and add them. Squeeze out the juice a little with a stick.

Fill up with the cold water. Garnish the rim of the glass with a strawberry.

AROMATIC HUGO PUNCH WITH STRAWBERRIES

Ingredients for 1 punch:

500 g strawberries
100 ml elderberry drink
4 tbsp fresh lime juice
2 limes
10 sprigs fresh mint
0.5 l cold water with carbonic acid
1 bottle of lemonade in "apple- elderflower" flavour
For the ice cubes:
½ bottle of lemonade in "apple elderflower" flavour
½ bottle of lemonade in "apple-rhubarb" flavour

Preparation:

Fill the two lemonades into ice cube moulds. Then put them in the freezer until they are frozen.

Now wash the strawberries, clean them and cut them into small cubes.

Then mix the cubes with the elderberry drink and the lime juice. Then place in the fridge for 30 minutes and leave to infuse.

Cut the two limes into thin slices. Then put the lime slices and the fresh mint in a large container.

Now fill up with cold mineral water and lemonade. It also works with dry sparkling wine if alcohol is desired.

Before serving, add homemade ice cubes to the punch.

SUMMER FLAMINGO COCKTAIL

Ingredients for 2 glasses:

12 cl orange juice
2 cl passion fruit juice
2 cl fresh lemon juice
2 cl grenadine
2 cl almond syrup
2 cl grapefruit juice
a few ice cubes
a few lemon slices

Preparation:

First, mix the orange juice, passion fruit juice, fresh lemon juice, grenadine, almond syrup and grapefruit juice in a shaker.

Fill the ice cubes and the lemon slices into two glasses.

Then add the drink and serve immediately.

HAWAIIAN LAVA FLOW COCKTAIL

Ingredients for 1 jar:

4 - 5 fresh strawberries
6 cl pineapple juice
6 cl cream
a dash of coconut syrup
some crushed ice

Preparation:

First, wash the strawberries and remove the leaves. Then puree them with a hand blender. If using frozen strawberries, add a little vanilla sugar.

Fill a glass one third full with the strawberry puree.

Now add crushed ice, pineapple juice, cream and coconut syrup to a shaker and shake vigorously. Shake until the cream is frothy.

Then pour the cream from the shaker onto the strawberry puree.

Stir the cream and the puree from the bottom to the top so that a nice pattern is formed.

If desired, place a strawberry on the edge for decoration.

APPLE COCKTAIL WITH CRANBERRY JUICE

Ingredients for 2 glasses:
50 g fresh raspberries
75 ml elderflower syrup
200 ml cranberry juice
250 ml apple juice
a few ice cubes
1 fresh lime

Preparation:
Mash the raspberries with a stick or simply with a fork.

Then pour the apple juice, elderflower syrup and cranberry juice into a shaker. Also add about 1/3 of the raspberry puree. Now shake thoroughly for a few seconds.

Now put the ice cubes and the rest of the puree into two tall glasses. Mix everything with the contents of the shaker. Then decorate both glasses with a slice of lime.

FITNESS COCKTAIL WITH FRESH FRUIT

Ingredients for 1 large carafe:
5 - 6 ice cubes
4 slices lemon
a handful of raspberries
cold mineral water to top up
a squeeze of lemon juice
a dash of raspberry syrup

Preparation:
First, fill the ice cubes into the carafe.

Cut 4 slices from a lemon and add them.

Then add a handful of raspberries and top up with the water.

Add a squeeze of fresh lemon and some raspberry syrup according to sweetness.

Stir well and leave to infuse for a few minutes.

Then pour the cocktail into larger glasses for serving.

LOVELY RIO COCKTAIL

Ingredients for 1 jar:

half a cup of orange juice
half a cup of lemonade
1 tablespoon grenadine
3 slices fresh lime
Some ice

Preparation:

First, fill some ice into your glass.

Then put the orange juice and lemonade in a shaker. Mix the ingredients well for about 15 seconds.

Then pour the cocktail into the glass with ice.

Then slowly pour in the grenadine around the rim of the glass.

Garnish the Rio cocktail with fresh lime slices and add more ice if desired.

HAPPY COCKTAIL WITH PASSION FRUIT

Ingredients for 1 jar:

200 ml cold non-alcoholic beer
100 ml cold passion fruit juice
1 - 2 tsp cold lemon juice or lime juice
some crushed ice
2 cl lemon juice
Grenadine

Preparation:

Fill a glass with the beer, passion fruit juice, and lime juice. Mix everything with a spoon. Then add the crushed ice.

Let some syrup - depending on the desired sweetness - run down the rim into the glass.

Garnish the cocktail with fresh lemon slices and serve the drink immediately.

REFRESHING SODA COCKTAIL FOR THE SUMMER

Ingredients for 1 jar:
Juice of half a lime
a few lime slices
some almond syrup
some grenadine syrup
Mineral water for refilling
1 fresh sprig of rosemary
Pomegranate seeds
a few large ice cubes

Preparation:
First, squeeze the juice of half a lime.

Finely slice the rest of the lime.

Then prepare a glass with a few large ice cubes.

Add the lime juice and stick in a sprig of rosemary.

Now add the pomegranate seeds to the glass and pour in enough cold mineral water.

Add syrup according to the desired sweetness.

Finally, decorate the refreshing drink with fresh lime slices.

FRUITY MANGO LASSI COCKTAIL

Ingredients for 1 jar:

250 g natural yoghurt (1.5 % fat)
150 ml milk
1 ripe mango
1 tsp lemon juice
1 tsp rose water
a little sugar to taste
some ice cream as desired
1 sprig of fresh mint for decoration

Preparation:

First, peel the mango and cut it into small cubes.

Then put the small cubes into a blender.

Add the other ingredients and mix everything very finely.

If desired, add some ice to the glass and pour in the cocktail. Garnish with some fresh mint if desired.

PINK BLUEBERRY LEMONADE COCKTAIL

Ingredients for 1 large pot:

1 cup water
1 cup sugar
1 cup lemon juice
1 cup blueberry juice
2 teaspoons of the zest of an untreated lemon
8 cups crushed ice
several slices of lemon

Preparation:

Take a shaker and put all the ingredients in it, except for the lemon slices.

First, shake everything vigorously for several seconds.

Pour the drink into a large jug or other container and place a few lemon slices inside. Add crushed ice to taste and serve the delicious drink immediately.

SWEET COCKTAIL WITH LIME

Ingredients for 1 jar:

10 - 12 fresh mint leaves
Juice from one lime
1 tablespoon sugar
12 cl cold mineral water
1 fresh slice of lemon or lime

Preparation:

First, cut one or more slices of a lime and pour them into a glass.

Add fresh mint leaves and crush the lime slices a little.

Then squeeze the juice from the lime and add it.

Now add the sugar - a little more if you like.

Fill up the drink with mineral water and enjoy it immediately.

DELICIOUS RASPBERRY COCKTAIL WITH ORANGE BLOSSOM

Ingredients for 2 glasses:

200 g raspberries
1 fresh lime
70 cl water with or without carbonic acid
100 g cane sugar
a few fresh mint leaves
1 teaspoon orange blossom water

Preparation:

First, cut the lime into small pieces and put them in a container.

Add the raspberries and mash the fruit a little so that juice comes out.

Then add the cane sugar and the fresh mint leaves.

Fill up with cold mineral water and add 1 teaspoon of orange blossom water. Stir everything again and then the refreshing drink can be served.

FRESH VIRGIN MANGO COLADA

Ingredients for 1 jar:

200 ml low-fat coconut milk
150 ml water
300 g frozen mango cubes
2 yellow peaches
1 tsp turmeric
1 small piece of ginger
1 pinch cayenne pepper
Juice of one orange
1 tsp maple syrup

Preparation:

First, peel the peaches and the ginger.

Put the mango, peaches, ginger, and all the other ingredients in a blender and blend until creamy.

Now dip the rim of a glass in water and then put it in a bowl with coconut flakes. This creates a beautiful white coconut rim on the glass.

Then pour the drink into the glass and decorate with some mango.

THIRST-QUENCHING CRODINO GINGER TONIC

Ingredients for 1 jar:

4 cl ginger syrup
2 cl fresh lime juice
100 ml orange juice
100 ml Crodino
100 ml tonic water
2 sprigs fresh mint
2 lime slices to garnish
some crushed ice

Preparation:

First, pour the ginger syrup, lime juice, and orange juice into a shaker and mix well.

Then add the crodino and stir once briefly.

Now fill two large glasses with crushed ice and divide the mixture between the glasses.

Pour 50 ml tonic water into both glasses and stir briefly.

Serve garnished with a sprig of fresh mint and a slice of lime.

MANGO COCKTAIL WITH FRESH MINT

Ingredients for 2 glasses:
¼ Mango
8 fresh mint leaves
1/3 lime
3 tbsp brown sugar
6 ice cubes
cold mineral water for infusion

Preparation:
Cut the mango into small pieces and put them into a blender. Puree the fruit to a fine pulp.

Now put the puree in a shaker with the mineral water and sugar and shake well.

First, pour the liquid into about two glasses.

Cut the lime into small pieces and add to the mixture.

Add a few ice cubes if desired and enjoy.

SUGAR-FREE BERRY COCKTAIL WITH WATERMELON

Ingredients for 2 glasses:

50 g raspberries
100 g strawberries
300 g watermelon
1 half untreated lime
1 handful of ice cubes
200 ml cold mineral water
1 handful fresh lemon balm

Preparation:

First, purée the raspberries and strawberries. Then pass through a sieve to remove the seeds.

Cut the watermelon into small pieces and add to the berry puree.

Squeeze the lime and puree everything again.

Place in the fridge until ready to serve.

When serving, fill each glass 1/3 full with the mixture. Then add mineral water and a few ice cubes.

The glasses can be decorated with fresh berries and some lemon balm. A strawberry is placed on the rim.

COLOURFUL FRUIT PUNCH

Ingredients for 1 jar:

3 l sparkling water
2 oranges
1 Apple
frozen raspberries
a few ice cubes

Preparation:

First, cut the oranges into rings and the apple into pieces.

Now pour the sparkling water into a large container and add the cut fruit with the frozen raspberries.

Add some more ice if you like.

Leave the punch to infuse, chilled, for a few hours until the water has turned a little pink.

NEW YEAR'S EVE COCKTAIL WITH STRAWBERRY JUICE

Ingredients for 1 jar:

2 cl mango juice
4 cl passion fruit juice
4 cl orange juice
3 cl strawberry juice
3 ice cubes
1 ½ cl coconut syrup
1 slice lemon

Preparation:

First, fill all the ingredients into a shaker together with the ice cubes. Shake everything thoroughly - preferably for one minute.

Then pour the cocktail into a suitable glass.

Decorate the cocktail with a slice of lemon and, if desired, a tinsel flag.

COCONUT YOGHURT COCKTAIL

Ingredients for 1 jar:

1 cup sweet natural yoghurt
½ cup coconut milk
2 tbsp coconut powder

Preparation:

Put all the ingredients in a shaker and shake well.

Then pour into a suitable glass and garnish with a little coconut powder if desired.

Depending on the consistency, the cocktail is better enjoyed with a spoon.

APPLE-CHERRY TONIC

Ingredients for 1 jar:

2 cl tonic water
1 cl apple juice
2 cl sour cherry nectar
1 squeeze of lime
2 sprigs fresh mint

Preparation:

First, fill a shaker with the cherry nectar. Then add a few ice cubes and the mint and shake for about 10 seconds.

Then pour the whole thing into a large glass. Fill it up with tonic water, the apple juice, and the squeeze of lime.

Finally, add a little mint to the glass for decoration.

GAUDY PRIMAVERA

Ingredients for 1 jar:

1 cl lemon juice
4 cl orange juice
4 cl passion fruit juice
4 cl grapefruit juice
2 cl grenadine
2 cocktail cherries
1 orange slice
Crushed ice or ice

Preparation:

In the first step, mix the grapfruit juice, the orange juice, and the lemon juice. Then add the grenadine and passion fruit juice and mix everything again in a shaker.

Add some ice or crushed ice.

Now fill a few ice cubes into a glass as desired and add the mixed cocktail.

Garnish the Primavera with a drinking straw, a slice of fresh orange, and the cocktail cherries.

DELICIOUS PEAR COCKTAIL

Ingredients for 1 jar:

for the rosemary syrup:
100 g granulated sugar
100 ml water
2 sprigs rosemary
For the cocktail:
3 cl pear juice
1 cl rosemary syrup
8 cl tonic water
1 pear
some cinnamon bark
Star anise
fresh thyme

Preparation:

First, we prepare a delicious rosemary syrup. Put all the ingredients for the syrup in a pot and bring to the boil.

The sugar should have dissolved completely. Then pull the pot aside and let the syrup cool.

Remove the rosemary sprigs and pour the homemade syrup through a coffee filter. Now put a few ice cubes in a glass.

Now add the rosemary syrup and the pear juice and mix everything together. Then top up with tonic water.

Wash a pear and cut it into slices. Put one slice in the glass.

Then serve with a cinnamon bark, star anise and a freshly plucked thyme leaf.

BORA BORA COCKTAIL

Ingredients for 1 jar:

4 cl coconut cream
6 cl pineapple juice
4 cl passion fruit juice
Grenadine
some crushed ice
Pineapple slices

Preparation:

Fill a glass with crushed ice.

Put all the other ingredients, except the grenadine, in a shaker and mix vigorously.

Pour the mixed cocktail into the glass and then slowly pour in the grenadine for a nice colour.

Decorate the glass with a few pineapple slices.

FRUITY-CREAMY GIN COCKTAIL

Ingredients for 1 jar:

100 g raspberries
2 tsp cane sugar
10 cl squeezed lemon juice
30 cl lemonade
a few ice cubes
fresh mint leaves for decoration

Preparation:

First, put a few ice cubes in a large glass.

Then add the sugar.

Fill the glass with lemonade and squeeze fresh lemon juice. Pour this into the glass.

Finally, decorate the finished drink with fresh mint leaves. Then enjoy immediately cold.

VITAMIN COCKTAIL WITH SEA BUCKTHORN

Ingredients for 1 jar:

50 ml sea buckthorn juice
200 ml pear juice
Juice of half an untreated lemon
a little zest of the lemon
1 tablespoon vanilla sugar
1 pinch up to ½ tsp cinnamon to taste
1 pear
Some ice

Preparation:

First, cut the pear into small pieces and put them on a skewer.

Pour some ice into a large glass.

Now put all the other ingredients in a blender and mix well.

Then pour the finished cocktail onto the ice and serve garnished with the fruit skewer.

RASPBERRY PUNCH WITH FRESH ROSEMARY

Ingredients for 4 glasses:
250 g raspberries
2 stalks rosemary
200 ml raspberry juice
4 tsp fresh lemon juice
Ice cubes or crushed ice
600 ml mineral water

Preparation:
First, wash the fresh raspberries. Then carefully dry them. Wash the fresh rosemary as well.

Now divide 200 g of raspberries between the 4 glasses and crush them to make the raspberry juice.

Now add the rosemary stems to the glasses and pour the fresh raspberry juice over everything. Then add a teaspoon of fresh lemon juice. Stir everything carefully and fill up with ice. Finally, add the mineral water and enjoy immediately cold.

EXOTIC SWIMMING POOL

Ingredients for 1 jar:

2 cl Blue Curacao (non-alcoholic)
2 cl coconut syrup
2 cl cream
14 cl pineapple juice

Preparation:

Put all the ingredients in a cocktail shaker or other blender. As an alternative, a container with a lid can also be used.

Then mix thoroughly for about 15 seconds. Then pour into a glass and decorate as desired.

Baking

GIN FIZZ GLAZE

You can use the gin fizz icing for any cake or pastry.

Ingredients:

1 lemon

1-2 cl gin

100-125 grams icing sugar

Preparation:

1. squeeze the lemon to get the juice. Try to have as few pieces of fruit as possible. It is best to still sieve the juice.

2. combine the lemon juice, gin and icing sugar and stir until the glaze appears smooth.

3. now you can spread the icing on your desired cake and let it set.

Hint:

A lemon cake is best, as the Gin Fizz glaze is prepared with lemon juice. In general, however, you can bake anything and glaze it with it.

GIN TONIC MUFFINS

As mentioned at the beginning of this book, you can do more with gin than just use it to mix cocktails. For example, these delicious gin and tonic muffins, which are perfect to bring along to a party.

Ingredients for the dough:

220 gram flour

3 tsp baking powder

200 gram sugar

1 sachet vanilla sugar

80 gram sour cream

100 ml gin

20 ml lime juice (preferably freshly squeezed)

125 gram butter

3 eggs

Salt

Preparation of the muffins:

1. let the butter warm up a little and also the eggs should not be fresh from the fridge (of course they should be fresh, but not cold). Mix the two together in a bowl.

2. in the next step, add the flour, baking powder and a little salt to the butter mixture and mix everything properly.

Then add the sour cream, gin and lime juice.

As with normal muffin baking, the batter should be nice and light to stir until you pour it into the muffin tins. While you are stirring, preheat the oven to 180 degrees Celsius.

Once the batter is ready, place the muffins in the oven for about 15 minutes. Since every oven is different, despite the heat setting, you should always check after ten minutes whether the muffins are already cooked through.

After the time in the oven, you can take the muffins out and leave them to cool. If you like to eat muffins like this, you can do so. Otherwise, read on for the icing.

The icing of these muffins is also made with gin.

Ingredients for the glaze:

200 grams icing sugar

Lime juice (preferably freshly squeezed)

Gin

Hint:

There are no quantities for the lime juice and gin, as this is best done according to your own taste and the consistency of the glaze.

Preparation of the icing:

First sieve the icing sugar so that the mixture does not form lumps.

2. once the icing sugar has been sifted into a bowl, carefully add the lime juice and gin.

3. you should taste the mixture again and again to make sure you like it. If the glaze is too strong, you can always add icing sugar and lime juice. You can also still add gin.

4. if the icing is to your liking, the muffins are now coated with it.

GIN AND TONIC TIRAMISU

Gin can also be used to make an excellent tiramisu. There are just about every kind of recipe you can imagine. This is also the case with gin.

Ingredients:

2 cl gin

2 cl tonic water

100 gram crème fraiche

50 gram natural yoghurt

80 ml cream

100 gram cream cheese

125 gram lady fingers

1 lime (optionally 1 lemon)

Icing sugar

Hint:

If you already have your own favourite tiramisu recipe, you can of course simply modify it and buy the ingredients.

Preparation:

The first step is to take care of the citrus fruit. Wash it, then grate the peel (about half of the fruit). You also take the juice from this half. Cut the other half into thin slices.

2. then you need to whip the cream until stiff.

3. now put all the ingredients together. First mix the cream cheese, crème fraiche, yoghurt, icing sugar and lime zest and some fruit juice.

4. then add the gin and tonic wate and gently fold in the cream.

5. at the end, sprinkle the ladyfingers with the remaining fruit juice. If the juice of the small fruit is not enough, you can squeeze another fruit.

6. once the biscuits are moist, place them in a baking dish and spread the mixture with gin over them. There are two layers, so make sure you have enough biscuits and cream for this.

7. at the end, garnish the tiramisu with the remaining shells and some fruit slices.

Chill and enjoy before eating.

GIN TONIC BISCUITS

As you can see, you can make a lot of things with gin. So can gin and tonic biscuits, which are perfect for a lovely girls' afternoon or even a guys' night out. They can even serve as nibbles for a romantic evening.

Ingredients:

7 cl gin

3 limes

400 gram flour

300 gram sugar

2 eggs

250 gram butter

200 ml tonic water

125 grams icing sugar

Salt

Preparation:

First you need to prepare the dough. To do this, take flour, 200 grams of sugar, the yolks of the eggs, salt and the butter and knead everything together until the dough is nice and soft.

In the next step, prepare the limes. To do this, grate the peels of the fruit and add them to the batter.

Then you have to wait, as the dough has to rest. To do this, you can wrap it in cling film or in a (clean) tea towel, which you moisten a little beforehand. Make sure that the dough is cold. The fridge is a better choice in summer, but the balcony or garden can also be used in winter.

After about half an hour, you can heat the oven and set it to 180 degrees convection. You will also need either baking paper for the baking tray or a reusable base, for example made of silicone.

While the oven is heating up, you can prepare everything else for the biscuits. Put a pot of tonic water on to boil and add the rest of the sugar. Finely slice the rest of the limes while you let the mixture steep in the pot for 3 minutes.

Now you can cut out the biscuits. Spread some flour generously on the work surface so that you can roll out the dough there and cut out the biscuits with your favourite shape. Place a slice of lime on each biscuit.

7. once this step is done, the biscuits first go into the oven for a quarter of an hour. During this time, you can mix the contents of the pot with gin and stir well.

8. after a quarter of an hour, you should remove the biscuits and drizzle with the mixture to taste.

Hint:

You can leave the biscuits in the oven afterwards, but remember that the alcohol will evaporate with the heat. It is better to wait a little longer until the biscuits are ready or have the colour you prefer.

Variant:

If the gin flavour on the icing is not enough for you, you can add some gin to the dough. To do this, it is best to use only drops at first and balance out the liquid with a little flour.

GIN TONIC CAKE (WITHOUT ICING)

I had already told you about the possibility of a gin fizz glaze. Now follows a recipe for a gin and tonic cake. Of course you can combine this with the glaze, just make sure that Gin Fizz and Gin Tonic, as you already know, are not the same thing.

Ingredients for the cake (without icing):

250 gram butter

5 eggs

Salt

350 grams flour (preferably wheat flour)

1 package baking powder

2 limes

4-5 cl gin

100 ml milk

Preparation:

Anyone who has baked a cake before should have no problem with this recipe. But don't worry, it's not too difficult even for beginners.

Before you start mixing the dough, preheat the oven to 1750 - 180 degrees Celsius. You can also grease and flour the loaf tin so that the cake is easy to remove from the tin after baking.

2 Let's move on to the dough. For this, put the butter in a bowl and stir it in advance until tender and creamy.

3. then add the eggs, a little salt, flour and baking powder.

Grate the zest from the limes and add this to the mix in the bowl. Also add the juice of the fruit.

Finally, add the milk and, of course, the gin.

Mix everything again and then spread the batter into the cake tin.

7. depending on the oven, bake the cake for about an hour.

Leave to cool and enjoy.

GIN AND TONIC ICE

In keeping with the motto "bake yourself an ice cream", there is actually also a recipe for a gin and tonic ice cream. It's not that surprising when you think of the simplicity behind it.

Ingredients:

60 ml gin

240 ml tonic water

25 grams icing sugar

30 ml lime juice (preferably freshly squeezed)

Limes

Popsicle mould (preferably popsicles)

Preparation:

First of all, the carbon dioxide must disappear completely from the tonic water. So open the bottle a few hours before preparation.

Hint:

If you need to do it quickly, you have two options: Pour the liquid into several glasses and stir with a spoon. Or shake the bottle vigorously from time to time. Open the lid carefully (!) and only a little, so that the carbon dioxide can escape. Repeat this process a few times.

Cut the limes into thin slices. Optionally, you can also remove the peel in advance.

Mix the gin, tonic water, lime juice and icing sugar together and divide the mixture between the ice moulds.

Once you have distributed them all, you can add the lime slices. Then your ice cream goes into the freezer.

5. after one hour, you should insert the sticks into the mould so that it does not sit on the edge of the ice cream` and you can eat from it without any problems.

6. now you have to be patient until the ice is frozen.

Cooking

GIN BBQ SAUCE

For a cosy barbecue and an exotic sauce for the next steak, this recipe is just right.

Ingredients:

150 ml gin

200 gram tomato paste

150 ml water

1 shallot

2 garlic cloves

8 chillies

4 tablespoons honey

Preparation:

Despite the many ingredients, the preparation is very simple and easy even for beginners.

1. place a saucepan on a stovetop and set it to the highest setting.

While the plate is heating up, put all the ingredients into the pot. You should roughly reduce the size of the vegetables in advance.

3. once the mixture boils, stir it every now and then and let it simmer for ten minutes.

At the end, when it has cooled down a little, put the mixture into a blender to chop the coarse vegetable pieces.

Pour into a container, seal and leave to cool until ready to grill.

PENNE WITH GIN

As you have already seen in the chapter "Baking", gin can be used in many ways. If you are not into sweets, I now have some pasta recipes for you.

Ingredients for 2 people:

250 gram penne

100 ml gin

1 tin of chopped tomatoes

1 tbsp tomato puree

1 onion

80 grams bacon cubes

Bouillon

Salt

Pepper

Parmesan

Preparation:

1. we start with the sauce, as this takes longer than the pasta. To start, you need to fry the bacon cubes. Do this in its own juices and add the onion (cut as small as possible).

2. when the bacon cubes change colour on all sides, add the tomato puree. To deglaze, add the tinned tomatoes and simmer the mixture with stock (not too much, but still to taste).

3. during this time you can put on pasta.

4 While the pasta water starts to boil, add the gin to the sauce. It must boil there for about 10 minutes so that most of the alcohol evaporates.

When the pasta is cooked, taste the sauce and season with salt and pepper. Remove from the heat and finish cooking the pasta now.

Serve the pasta with the sauce and parmesan.

SUMMER PASTA WITH GIN

There is also a delicious paste recipe for those warm days when you can't even think about cooking.

Ingredients for 2 people:

250 gram pasta

100 gram tomato paste

1 lemon

1 shallot

1 garlic

80 ml gin

1 tsp chilli flakes

100 ml cream

15 gram butter

Olive oil

Parmesan

Salt

Pepper

Basil leaves

Preparation:

1. first put the pasta on according to the instructions on the packet.

While the water starts to simmer, cut the lemon in half. Place one half in the pan, cut side down, and fry. Once caramelised, set aside.

3. always watch the pasta water. While doing this, now chop the shallot.

Sauté the shallot pieces until they are translucent and add the garlic and chilli flakes.

Then add tomato paste to the pan and simmer until the sauce is nice and red. Deglaze the sauce with gin.

6. continue to watch the pasta and now add the cream to the pan.

After everything has simmered a little, season with salt and pepper and finally add the butter.

Add a little of the pasta water to the sauce when the pasta is cooked.

Drain the pasta and quickly add it to the pan, which you will now stop heating.

10. now add the juice of the lemon you had in the pan at the beginning, as well as parmesan.

Pull out and leave to cool.

Season again before serving, adding salt and pepper if necessary.

13. offer pieces of parmesan and basil leaves to eat with the dish.

HERB BUTTER WITH GIN

You can not only conjure up wonderful dishes with gin, but also and above all use it to make sauces, butter or jam. For example, a herb butter that you will love.

Ingredients:

60 ml gin

1 cucumber

400 gram butter

1 bunch chives

Fresh parsley if desired

Preparation:

1. first wash the cucumber and then cut it into small cubes. Alternatively, you can grate the cucumber.

2. now add the cucumber pieces to the gin and leave to infuse for about 10 minutes.

Meanwhile, you can already chop the chives and optionally the parsley.

If 10 minutes have not yet passed, you can warm the butter in a pan. Make sure that nothing burns.

5. add the herbs and the cucumber and turn off the heat on the cooker while you mix everything.

Season and leave to cool.

7. then chill properly and serve for dinner.

JAM WITH GIN

Gin doesn't necessarily have to be missing from breakfast either. There are wonderful recipes for jam. I present two examples below.

Berry Jam with Gin

The berry jam with gin has few ingredients and is very easy to make. If you have never made jam before, this is a recipe you should try without hesitation. I present blackberry jam, but you can use your favourite berries.

Ingredients:

5 cl gin

1 kilo blackberries

1 kilo jam sugar

Preparation:

1. make sure that the berries are free from insect remains and also have no soft or spoiled spots.

Wash the berries and let the water drain off completely as well as possible.

3. mash the berries and put the liquid as well as the pieces into a large pot.

4. add the preserving sugar and let it simmer while stirring.

Boil vigorously for 4 minutes.

Turn off the heat on the cooker and add the gin.

7. as soon as the mixture has cooled down a little, pour the jam into jars and leave them sealed to cool completely.

GOOSEBERRY JAM WITH GIN AND TONIC

Another jam recipe also serves only as an example of what you can conjure up with the breakfast spread and gin.

Ingredients:

5 cl gin

900 gram gooseberries

350 tonic water

500 grams jam sugar

Lemon juice from two freshly squeezed lemons

Preparation:

Wash the gooseberries and put them in a large pot.

Add the preserving sugar.

3. puree this mixture.

4. then add the tonic water and lemon juice and bring everything to the boil.

5. Boil vigorously for 4 minutes.

Turn off the heat on the cooker and add the gin.

7. as soon as the mixture has cooled down a little, pour the jam into jars and leave them sealed to cool completely.

Hint:

As you will notice, this recipe is hardly any different from the jam, especially in the preparation. It is mainly the quantities of the ingredients that make the difference. You can also vary the berries in this recipe.

CREAM CHEESE WITH GIN

To finish off the breakfast recipes, I would like to show you the simple way to make cream cheese with gin.

Ingredients:

250 gram cream cheese

3 tsp jam

Optionally fresh mint

3 cl gin

Preparation:

Since it is not cooked here, but mixed with existing ingredients, the preparation is extremely simple.

Simply blend all the ingredients until the mixture is creamy and chill.

Hint:

If you add mint, it must be chopped in advance.

SELF-PRODUCTION

Normally, gin is distilled, which neither you nor I can do in our own homes. Nevertheless, you can make your own gin, as there is a variety that does not require distillation. Moreover, the necessary things are either all already in the house or you can quickly buy the necessary material together in the nearest supermarket.

Enclosed you will find the shopping list:

Juniper berries

1 litre vodka

1 empty glass bottle

1 Funnel

1 sieve

Coffee filter

Spices

Even at first glance, you realise that it can't be that difficult to make your own gin.

Step by step guide:

The first step is child's play. Simply add the juniper berries and the vodka. Now you have to wait so that the berries can release the aroma. This takes about a day, during which you should keep the bottle sealed, dry and protected from light.

After you have waited a day, spices are added. Ultimately, you can decide which note you want your gin to have. If you want to start with a classic variant, I recommend cardamom or citrus peel. You can also add the botanicals mentioned at the beginning. Now it's time to wait again.

3. so you've already managed two steps and spent an estimated two days more waiting than working on your gin. It's time to taste. Now you have the chance to decide whether you already like the taste or whether

you want to add more seasoning and other ingredients. If you decide on the former, we will continue with step 4. If you still want to change something, you will have to wait a little longer. This time, however, not too long. Keep tasting in the meantime.

Once the gin has the desired aroma, you need to filter it. The best way to do this is to use the sieve in which you place two coffee filters. Slowly pour the mixture into the sieve and let the drops run into the desired container.

When it is finally done, you can taste it again, but your gin is not yet ready. It still needs a little time to rest. Allow it that and let the gin sit for about a week before you enjoy your own gin.

Imprint

2023

ISBN: 9798389933941

1st edition

Contact: Markus Mägerle/ Am Kreisgraben 17/ 93104 Riekofen/ Germany

Printed in Great Britain
by Amazon

34985577R00126